Leckie×Leckie
Scotland's leading educational publishers

Success guides

HIGHER
Biology

✕ Fred Thornhill ✕

ISBN 978-1-84372-721-7

Published by
Leckie & Leckie
An imprint of HarperCollins*Publishers*
Westerhill Road, Bishopbriggs, Glasgow, G64 2QT
T: 0844 576 8126 F: 0844 576 8131
leckieandleckie@harpercollins.co.uk www.leckieandleckie.co.uk

Special thanks to
Planman Technologies (creative packaging and illustration),
Helen Bleck (copy-edit), Janet Fisher (proofread)

A CIP Catalogue record for this book is available from the British Library.

Unit 1 – Cell Biology

Unit 2 – Genetics and adaptation

Variation

Unit 3 – Control and regulation

Control of growth and development

Cell variety

Cell organisation

The bodies of organisms are built of cells. Some organisms consist of just one cell (**unicellular**) and others consist of many cells (**multicellular**).

In multicellular organisms, cells of the same type and performing the same function are organised into **tissues**.

Several different tissues with related functions group together to form an **organ**.

Different organs can be combined into a major **system**.

Together the systems, organs and tissues make up the **organism**.

Cells are small and can only be seen clearly with a microscope. Detailed cell structure can only be seen with an electron microscope.

All cells typically have an outer **plasma membrane,** which forms the active boundary of the cell. Movement of materials into and out of the cell is controlled by the membrane. The membrane encloses the fluid **cytoplasm** in which are many small structures (**organelles**). These carry out the essential processes of the cell. The largest organelle is the **nucleus** which contains the genetic information of the cell.

Plant cells also have a structural **cell wall** outside the plasma membrane and they have a large **vacuole**, containing cell sap, in the cytoplasm. Cells in the green parts of plants also contain **chloroplasts** in the cytoplasm.

These features can be seen using a light microscope but other organelles can only be seen with an electron microscope.

The ultrastructure of cells

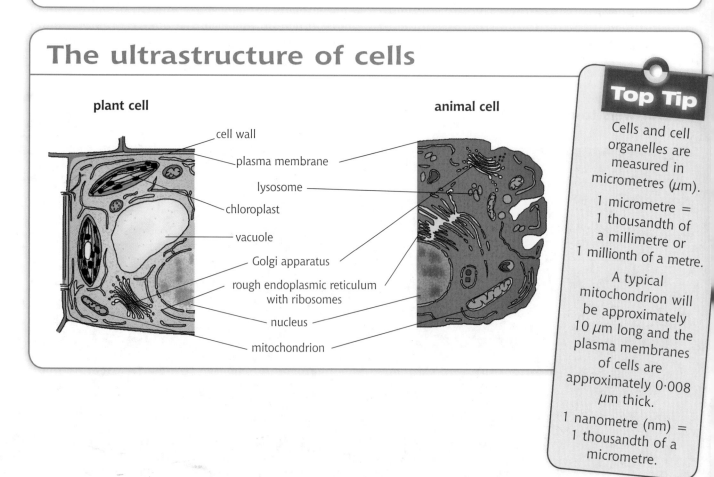

plant cell

animal cell

- cell wall
- plasma membrane
- lysosome
- chloroplast
- vacuole
- Golgi apparatus
- rough endoplasmic reticulum with ribosomes
- nucleus
- mitochondrion

Top Tip

Cells and cell organelles are measured in micrometres (μm).

1 micrometre = 1 thousandth of a millimetre or 1 millionth of a metre.

A typical mitochondrion will be approximately 10 μm long and the plasma membranes of cells are approximately 0·008 μm thick.

1 nanometre (nm) = 1 thousandth of a micrometre.

Specialised cells

Although cells have the same basic components, they do vary according to the specialised functions they perform.

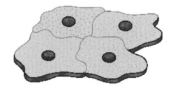

epithelial cells – These cells are flattened. They form protective linings in air passages and the gut.

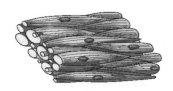

smooth muscle cells – These cells have contractile fibres and they form sheets, for example in the wall of the gut where they are responsible for peristalsis.

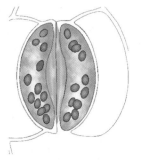

guard cells – These are curved cells with thickened walls on the inner surface. This helps to produce their change in shape, which results in the opening and closing of the stomata.

phloem cells – These cells have perforated end walls and continuous strands of cytoplasm running through them. These help transport food along the sieve tubes.

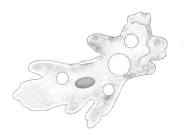

unicellular amoeba – This organism is able to move and feed by causing its cytoplasm to flow. It feeds by flowing around organic material and engulfing it.

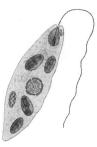

unicellular euglena – This free-swimming organism contains chloroplasts and carries out photosynthesis. It possesses an eye spot which can distinguish between light and dark.

Quick Test 1

1. What is meant by the terms **unicellular** and **multicellular** when referring to living organisms?
2. The cells which make up sieve tubes in the phloem of plants do not possess nuclei.
   How does this feature contribute to the function of the cells?
3. What benefit does the euglena gain from having an eye spot?

Absorption and secretion of materials

Movement by diffusion

The molecules of all liquids and gases move around. This causes them to spread and results in the process of **diffusion**. Diffusion is the movement of molecules from a region of high concentration to a region of lower concentration. This is sometimes referred to as movement down a concentration gradient. It will continue until the molecules become evenly spread. Movement of molecules by diffusion into or out of a cell does not require any energy expenditure by the cell.

Movement by osmosis

Osmosis is the movement of **water** molecules from a region of high concentration to a region of lower concentration through a **selectively permeable membrane**. Therefore, osmosis is a particular case of diffusion. Movement of water by osmosis into or out of a cell does not require any energy expenditure by the cell.

Solutions with a high water concentration are said to be **hypotonic** to solutions with a lower water concentration.

Solutions with a low water concentration are said to be **hypertonic** to solutions with a higher water concentration.

Solutions with equal water concentrations are said to be **isotonic** to each other.

Osmosis can cause changes to cells.

The table shows the effects of placing cells in different concentrations of solution.

> **Top Tip**
>
> Remember that the terms **hypertonic** and **hypotonic** refer to the concentration of solute in a solution, not the concentration of water. If one solution is hypertonic compared with another, it will have a higher solute concentration but a lower water concentration.

Cell type	Surrounding solution	Water movement by osmosis	Effect on cell
animal	hypertonic	leaves cell	Cell shrinks
	hypotonic	enters cell	Cell swells and bursts
plant	hypertonic	leaves cell	Cytoplasm and vacuole shrink. Membrane pulls away from cell wall. Cell becomes plasmolysed
	hypotonic	enters cell	Cell swells. It is prevented from bursting by the cell wall

When plant cells gain water, the tissue feels firmer and is described as being **turgid**.

When plant cells lose water, the tissue feels soft and wilted. It is described as being **flaccid**.

Movement by active transport

The movement of many molecules into or out of cells takes place from regions of low concentrations to regions of higher concentrations. This is movement against the concentration gradient and it does not take place by diffusion. Such movement does require energy released by respiration to make it happen.

The movement of molecules into or out of a cell from a low to a higher concentration is called **active transport**.

Many molecules are too large to pass through cell membranes by diffusion. However, they can still be transported across cell membranes by the action of some membrane proteins. This type of movement also requires energy expenditure by the cell and is another example of active transport.

Cell walls and plasma membranes

Plant cell walls are made of **cellulose fibres**. Cellulose is synthesised from glucose. Its fibres are strong and help support the plant. Cell walls are fully permeable to the movement of materials and are not involved in controlling what enters or leaves the cell.

The plasma membranes of cells are made of **proteins** and **phospholipids**. The phospholipid molecules form double-layered sheets which are stable but fluid. Different types of protein molecules are embedded in the phospholipid sheets and these proteins give the membrane its properties. The proteins can move in the fluid-like phospholipid layers. Some proteins are enzymes, some form pores for the passage of small molecules, some actively transfer materials from one side of the membrane to the other and some control the movement and shape of the membrane. This type of membrane structure is called the **fluid-mosaic model**.

The plasma membrane is selectively permeable and allows the passage of water by osmosis, and other small molecules by diffusion. However, the membrane plays an active role in enabling the passage of many substances and preventing the passage of others. Diffusion and osmosis do not require energy expenditure by the cell, but active transport of substances across the membrane does require energy.

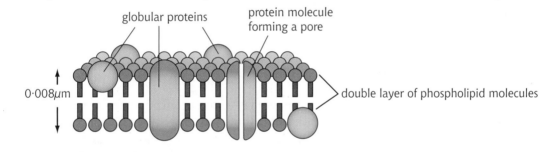

Quick Test 2

1. The graph shows the effect of changing oxygen concentration on the concentration of potassium ions inside a mammalian cell.

   (a) Explain the shape of the graph between oxygen concentrations of 1·0 and 2·0 units.
   (b) Suggest a reason why the graph levels off at oxygen concentrations above 3·0 units.

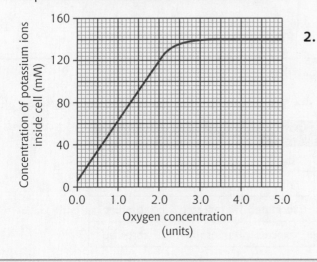

2.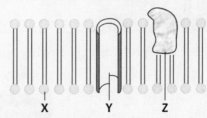

   The diagram shows a section through a plasma membrane.
   (a) Identify the molecules labelled X and Z on the diagram.
   (b) Describe the role of the molecule labelled Y on the diagram.

The role of light and photosynthetic pigments

Role of chlorophyll *a* and other pigments

When light reaches a leaf some bounces off the leaf (**reflection**), some passes through the leaf (**transmission**) and some is taken into the leaf (**absorption**). Only absorbed light may be used in photosynthesis.

A leaf appears green because the green part of the light spectrum is reflected or transmitted by the leaf. Other parts of the spectrum are absorbed by the leaf. This is confirmed by the **absorption spectrum** for **chlorophyll a**, which shows how strongly different wavelengths of light are absorbed.

Absorption spectrum for chlorophyll a

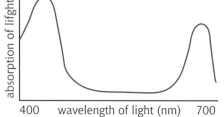

This shows that the pigment **chlorophyll a** absorbs most effectively at wavelengths 400–500 nm (blue) and 700 nm (red). There is very little absorption of the in between green – yellow wavelengths

If the actual rate of photosynthesis is measured at different wavelengths of light, the **action spectrum** of a plant can be seen.

Action spectrum for a plant

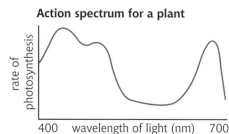

The pattern is similar to the absorption spectrum for chlorophyll *a*, but not identical to it. It shows that the plant can carry out photosynthesis using wavelengths of light that are not absorbed by chlorophyll *a*.

This is because other pigments are present which can also absorb light. These include: **carotene, xanthophyll** and **chlorophyll b**. The additional pigments are called **accessory pigments**. They enable plants to broaden their absorption spectrum by absorbing light from a much wider range of wavelengths than chlorophyll *a* alone. The absorbed energy is then passed to chlorophyll *a* for use in photosynthesis.

Quick Test 3

1. The diagram below represents light striking a leaf.

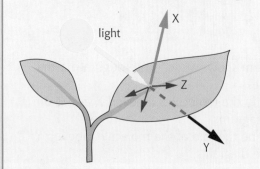

Which of the following describes the possible fates of the light?

Answer	X	Y	Z
A	absorbed	transmitted	reflected
B	reflected	absorbed	transmitted
C	transmitted	reflected	absorbed
D	reflected	transmitted	absorbed

Separating photosynthetic pigments

The various pigments present in plant leaves can be separated and identified by **chromatography**.

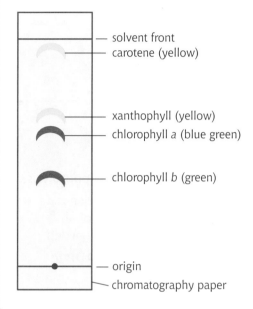

- solvent front
- carotene (yellow)
- xanthophyll (yellow)
- chlorophyll *a* (blue green)
- chlorophyll *b* (green)
- origin
- chromatography paper

- Leaves are cut up and crushed in a solvent such as propanone.
- The crushed material is filtered to give a clear green filtrate containing the leaf pigments.
- The filtrate is carefully 'spotted' onto a marked origin on chromatography paper.
- The bottom edge of the chromatography paper is dipped into a different solvent, such as a propanone/petroleum ether mixture, with the origin just above the solvent surface.
- The solvent is allowed to run up the paper past the spot of pigments.
- As it does so, the pigments are carried upwards at different speeds because of differences in their solubility, and so become separated.
- The relative distance each pigment is carried is used to identify it.
- Different solvents will produce different patterns of separation.

Chloroplast structure

Photosynthesis takes place in **chloroplasts**. These organelles are found in the cytoplasm of cells in the green parts of plants. Photosynthesis takes place in two stages within the chloroplasts.

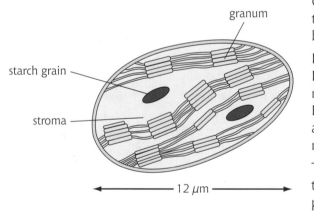

- granum
- starch grain
- stroma

← 12 μm →

Chloroplasts are small organelles that have a double membrane boundary.

Inside is a fluid called the **stroma**. In the stroma are disc-shaped membranes arranged in stacks. Each stack is called a **granum** and the grana are linked by other membranes.

The grana and the stroma are the sites of the two stages of photosynthesis.

Top Tip

Remember that chloroplasts are not found in all plant cells. Even in green leaves, chloroplasts are only found in the palisade mesophyll, spongy mesophyll and the guard cells.

---

2. The diagram below represents the absorption of different colours of light by a photosynthetic pigment.

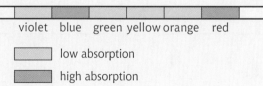

violet   blue   green   yellow   orange   red

◻ low absorption

▨ high absorption

(a) Name this photosynthetic pigment.

(b) State the role of the accessory pigments in photosynthesis.

The stages of photosynthesis

The location and significance of the light-dependent stage

The light-dependent stage of photosynthesis takes place on the grana of the chloroplasts. The photosynthetic pigments are present on the membranes of the grana. Light is absorbed by all the pigments and the energy transferred to the chlorophyll *a* molecules.

Some of this energy is used to split water molecules into hydrogen and oxygen – a process called **photolysis**.

Some of the energy is used to build up molecules of **ATP** (adenosine triphosphate) from **ADP** (adenosine diphosphate) and inorganic phosphate groups (Pi). ATP is important in the energy management of all cells. It is built up whenever energy is available and then breaks down to release its energy whenever needed.

The hydrogen from photolysis becomes attached to a hydrogen acceptor compound called **NADP** to form **NADPH**.

NADPH and ATP are the important products of the light-dependent stage. The oxygen from photolysis is a by-product and diffuses out of the leaves.

The location and significance of carbon fixation (the Calvin cycle)

The second stage of photosynthesis takes place in the liquid stroma of the chloroplasts. It depends on the NADPH and ATP from the first stage and, although it does not need light, it will only continue in darkness until these run out.

This stage is called **carbon fixation** or the **Calvin cycle**. It involves the chemical reduction of carbon dioxide to carbohydrate by the addition of hydrogen. The hydrogen is obtained from the NADPH. The reactions also need the energy from ATP.

The essential steps of carbon fixation are:

- the reaction of carbon dioxide with a 5-carbon compound **RuBP** (ribulose biphosphate) to form two molecules of a 3-carbon compound **GP** (glycerate phosphate)
- the reduction of GP by hydrogen from NADPH in reactions using energy from ATP
- the formation of replacement RuBP and some carbohydrate by these reactions
- the removal of the carbohydrate to form glucose.

Top Tip

You must be able to name the following chemicals involved in photosynthesis and say what they do:

ADP ATP NADP NADPH GP RuBP

In all cases, the abbreviations are enough. You do not need to use the full name. You should know how many carbon atoms are present in molecules of GP and RuBP.

Summary of photosynthesis

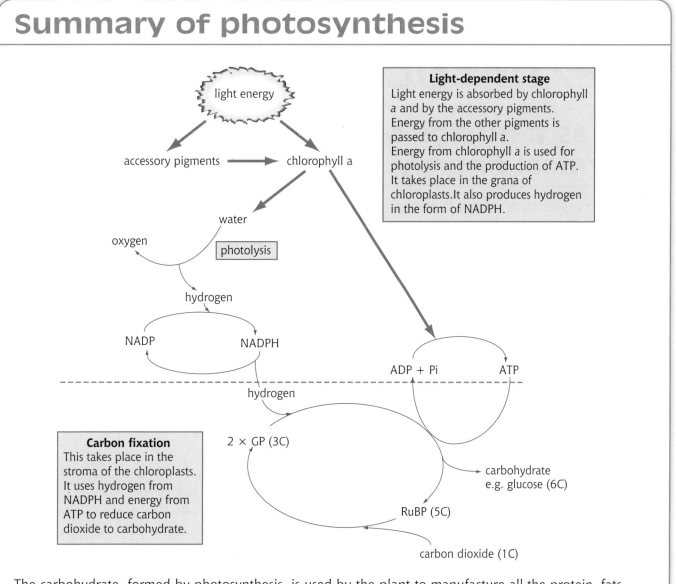

Light-dependent stage
Light energy is absorbed by chlorophyll a and by the accessory pigments. Energy from the other pigments is passed to chlorophyll a.
Energy from chlorophyll a is used for photolysis and the production of ATP. It takes place in the grana of chloroplasts. It also produces hydrogen in the form of NADPH.

Carbon fixation
This takes place in the stroma of the chloroplasts. It uses hydrogen from NADPH and energy from ATP to reduce carbon dioxide to carbohydrate.

The carbohydrate, formed by photosynthesis, is used by the plant to manufacture all the protein, fats, nucleic acids and other organic compounds it needs.

Quick Test 4

1. (a) Name the element resulting from photolysis that is needed for the carbon fixation stage of photosynthesis.
   (b) In what form does this element enter the carbon fixation stage?
   (c) What is the function of this element in the carbon fixation stage?
2. (a) Name two chemicals produced from GP during the carbon fixation stage of photosynthesis.
   (b) Which of these chemicals is needed to maintain the Calvin cycle?

The importance of ATP/mitochondria

ATP as a means of transferring chemical energy

ATP has already been mentioned as being produced during the light-dependent stage of photosynthesis, using energy absorbed by chlorophyll, and then passing that energy to the carbon fixation stage.

ATP is also produced using energy released by the breakdown of glucose during respiration.

ATP is built up from ADP and inorganic phosphate whenever energy is available, for example during the light-dependent stage of photosynthesis and during respiration. The ATP then breaks down whenever energy is needed to drive other reactions in cells which require energy.

The amount of energy released by the breakdown of a molecule of ATP is relatively small and is convenient for the energy-requiring reactions of the cell.

When ATP breaks down, ADP is re-formed and can be built back up into ATP when more energy becomes available. This cycle takes place continually in cells.

Cyclic reactions like this are efficient because the necessary raw materials are continually being re-formed and reused.

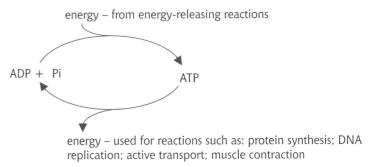

energy – from energy-releasing reactions

ADP + Pi   ATP

energy – used for reactions such as: protein synthesis; DNA replication; active transport; muscle contraction

Mitochondria

The initial stage of respiration takes place in the cell cytoplasm but the later stages of aerobic respiration take place in cell organelles called **mitochondria**.

A mitochondrion has a double membrane. The inner membrane layer has folds called **cristae** and the middle of a mitochondrion is a fluid-filled region called the **matrix**.

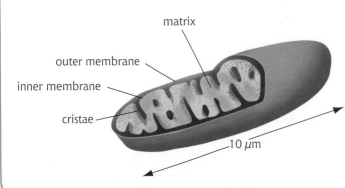

matrix

outer membrane

inner membrane

cristae

10 μm

The reactions of the Krebs cycle take place in the fluid-filled matrix of the mitochondrion.

The hydrogen-carrier molecules of the cytochrome system are located on the membranes of the cristae and so these reactions take place on the surface of these membranes.

Stages of respiration

Glycolysis

This is the first stage for all forms of respiration, both aerobic and anaerobic. **Glycolysis** does not require oxygen. It takes place in the cytoplasm of cells and involves the breakdown of glucose molecules into **pyruvic acid**. The essential points about glycolysis are:

- enzymes and two molecules of ATP are needed to start the reaction
- 6-carbon glucose molecules are broken down into two molecules of 3-carbon pyruvic acid
- enough energy is released to produce four ATP molecules (a net gain of two ATP) for each glucose molecule
- hydrogen is also released and combines with the hydrogen acceptor **NAD** to form **NADH**
- fats and proteins may be used but glucose is the main respiratory substrate.

Top Tip

Once again, you must know the names of some of the chemicals involved and what they do:

pyruvic acid; acetyl group; citric acid; NAD; NADH; cytochrome enzymes; ATP; ADP.

You should also know the number of carbon atoms present in molecules of pyruvic acid, acetyl group, citric acid.

Krebs cycle (citric acid cycle)

This is one of the aerobic stages of respiration. It takes place as a continuation of glycolysis only if oxygen is available. It takes place in the fluid-filled central matrix of cell organelles called **mitochondria**.

The steps of **Krebs cycle** are:

- 3-carbon pyruvic acid is broken down to a 2-carbon **acetyl** group
- the acetyl group combines with coenzyme A (CoA) to form **acetyl CoA**
- the acetyl group reacts with a 4-carbon compound to form 6-carbon **citric acid**
- citric acid is converted back to the 4-carbon compound by the loss of carbon dioxide and hydrogen
- the hydrogen combines with the hydrogen carrier NAD to form NADH
- NADH passes the hydrogen to the final stage of respiration, the cytochrome system on the **cristae** of the mitochondria
- each step is controlled by enzymes.

The cytochrome system

The **cytochrome system** consists of a series of hydrogen acceptor molecules and it takes place on the cristae, of the mitochondria. The steps of the cytochrome system are:

- the first cytochrome hydrogen acceptor receives hydrogen from NADH
- the hydrogen is passed from one hydrogen acceptor to another several times in a series
- energy is released by each hydrogen transfer and used to build up ATP from ATP + Pi
- oxygen acts as the final hydrogen acceptor to produce water.

If no oxygen is available, the reactions of the Krebs cycle and the cytochrome system cannot take place. In this case, the ATP from glycolysis is all that is produced. It is the hydrogen transfer reactions of the cytochrome system that release most of the energy from respiration and lead to the production of most ATP.

For each glucose molecule broken down, glycolysis produces a net gain of two molecules of ATP. The cytochrome system produces thirty-six molecules of ATP, giving a total of thirty-eight molecules of ATP.

Summary of respiration

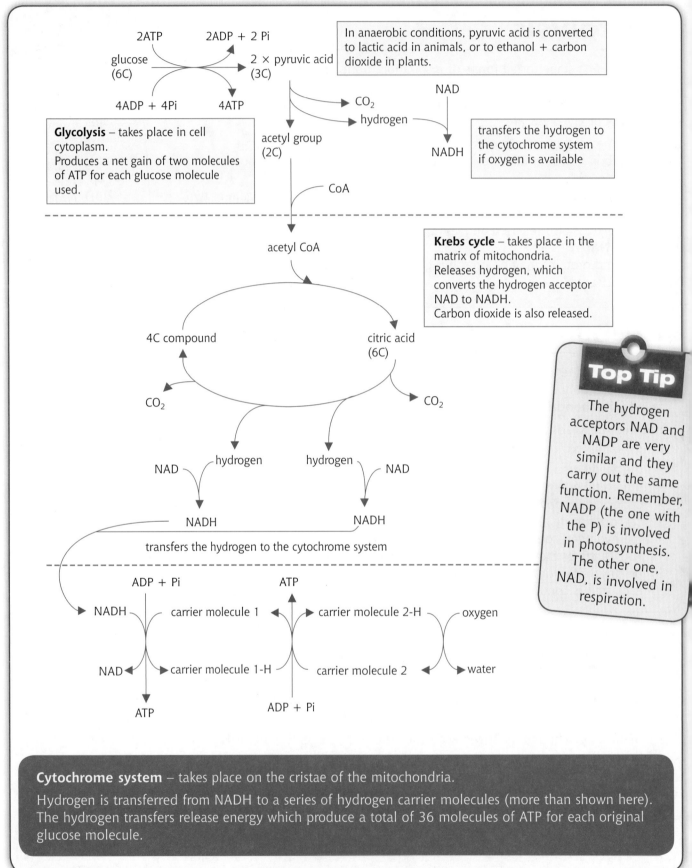

In anaerobic conditions, pyruvic acid is converted to lactic acid in animals, or to ethanol + carbon dioxide in plants.

Glycolysis – takes place in cell cytoplasm.
Produces a net gain of two molecules of ATP for each glucose molecule used.

transfers the hydrogen to the cytochrome system if oxygen is available

Krebs cycle – takes place in the matrix of mitochondria.
Releases hydrogen, which converts the hydrogen acceptor NAD to NADH.
Carbon dioxide is also released.

Top Tip

The hydrogen acceptors NAD and NADP are very similar and they carry out the same function. Remember, NADP (the one with the P) is involved in photosynthesis. The other one, NAD, is involved in respiration.

transfers the hydrogen to the cytochrome system

Cytochrome system – takes place on the cristae of the mitochondria.

Hydrogen is transferred from NADH to a series of hydrogen carrier molecules (more than shown here). The hydrogen transfers release energy which produce a total of 36 molecules of ATP for each original glucose molecule.

Differences between aerobic and anaerobic respiration

These are summarised in the table.

Feature	Aerobic respiration	Anaerobic respiration
Number of ATP molecules gained for each molecule of glucose	38	2
Final breakdown products	carbon dioxide + water	lactic acid (in bacteria and animals) ethanol + carbon dioxide (in plants and fungi)

Quick Test 5

1. Describe the role of ATP in metabolism.
2. It is estimated that the amount of ATP present in the body of an average human male remains remarkably constant at about 50 g. Explain why this is so.
3. The inner membrane of the mitochondrion is folded to form the cristae. What is the benefit of this feature?
4. Give an account of respiration under the following headings:
   (a) glycolysis
   (b) the Krebs cycle

Proteins and DNA

The functional variety of proteins

All proteins are built up from the same 20 amino acids organised in chains.

The sequence of amino acids in a protein chain is of great importance because this determines the shape of the protein molecule. The shape of the protein molecule determines its type and function.

There are two general categories of proteins, **fibrous** and **globular**.

The chains of fibrous proteins form long parallel strands which have great strength. Fibrous proteins have structural functions. Examples are keratin, which is found in skin, fingernails, hair and feathers, and collagen, which is found in bones, tendons and ligaments.

Globular proteins have chains which are folded to give molecules with three-dimensional shapes. The shapes of the molecules give them particular chemical properties and they function as enzymes, hormones and antibodies.

DNA structure

Deoxyribonucleic acid (**DNA**) is the chemical from which chromosomes are made. Therefore DNA forms the genetic material of a cell.

A DNA molecule is a chain of many millions of smaller molecules called **nucleotides**. Each nucleotide has three parts, **deoxyribose** sugar, a phosphate group and an organic **base**. There are four different bases and so there are four different nucleotides.

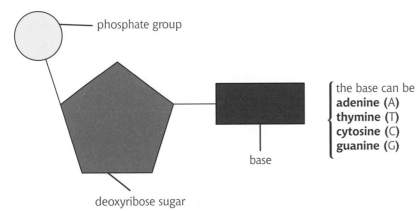

phosphate group

the base can be
adenine (A)
thymine (T)
cytosine (C)
guanine (G)

base

deoxyribose sugar

The nucleotides are linked together by strong chemical bonds between their sugar and phosphate groups to form long chains. Nucleotide bases are able to form weak hydrogen bonds with each other in very specific pairings.

Adenine always pairs with thymine and cytosine always pairs with guanine.

DNA exists as two parallel chains linked together by these base pairs.

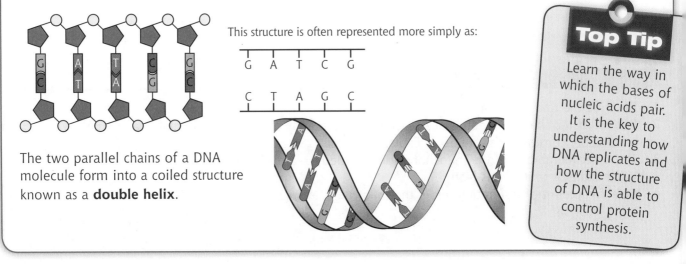

The two parallel chains of a DNA molecule form into a coiled structure known as a **double helix**.

This structure is often represented more simply as:

G   A   T   C   G

C   T   A   G   C

Top Tip

Learn the way in which the bases of nucleic acids pair. It is the key to understanding how DNA replicates and how the structure of DNA is able to control protein synthesis.

DNA replication

When cells divide, the chromosomes must be replicated so that daughter cells can receive a full complement of chromosomes. Chromosome replication happens because of the base-pairing ability of DNA, ensuring that genetic information is unchanged from parent cell to daughter cells.

DNA replication involves a number of stages.

- Parallel strands of the double helix untwist and separate or unzip by the breaking of the weak hydrogen bonds between paired bases.
- Single free nucleotides in the cell become aligned against complementary exposed bases of the DNA chains, according to the base-pairing rules.
- Single nucleotides link together between their phosphate and sugar groups to form new complementary chains with each of the original chains.
- Two double helixes form, identical to each other and to the original.

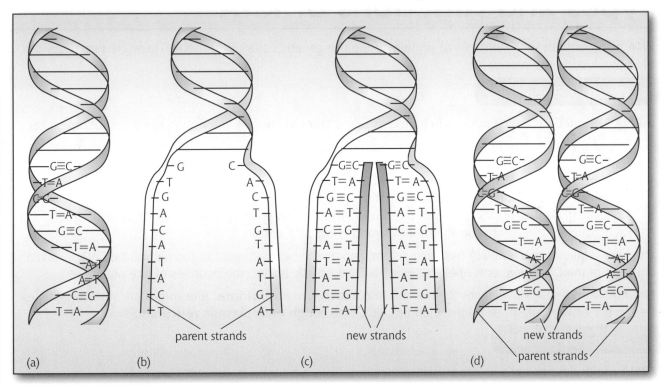

(a) (b) parent strands (c) new strands (d) new strands parent strands

DNA replication requires free nucleotides and the original DNA strands to act as templates. It also requires appropriate enzymes called DNA polymerase and ATP to provide the chemical energy for the process.

DNA replication means that the genetic information of a cell is doubled. Each chromosome becomes a pair of identical chromatids, ready to be separated and shared between daughter cells during mitosis.

Each chromosome contains many genes. A gene is a region of a chromosome in which the sequence of bases forms a code which controls the synthesis of a particular protein. Since proteins have so many vital functions in cells, the control of protein synthesis controls the growth, development and activities of a cell.

Quick Test 6

1. Free DNA nucleotides are needed for DNA replication.
   Name one other substance that is needed for DNA replication.
2. A single strand of a DNA molecule has 6000 nucleotides of which 24% are adenine and 18% are cytosine.
   (a) Calculate the combined percentage of thymine and guanine bases on the same DNA strand.
   (b) How many guanine bases would be present on the complementary strand of this DNA molecule?

RNA

Differences between DNA and RNA

Ribonucleic acid (**RNA**) is similar in structure to DNA, but there are important differences.

- RNA is single-stranded, DNA is double-stranded.
- RNA is a small molecule compared with DNA.
- RNA contains the sugar ribose, DNA contains deoxyribose sugar.
- RNA contains the base **uracil** instead of thymine. Both form base pairs with adenine.

Types and functions of RNA

RNA is important in the synthesis of proteins using the genetic code of the DNA. There are two types of RNA involved in the process.

1. Messenger RNA (mRNA)

mRNA is formed in the cell nucleus in a process called **transcription**. Transcription has a number of stages:

- Part of the DNA double helix of a chromosome untwists and separates or unzips. This part contains a gene which codes for a particular protein.
- Bases of one of the DNA chains are exposed.
- Complementary RNA nucleotides become aligned opposite the exposed DNA bases.
- Adjacent RNA nucleotides join to form an mRNA chain that is complementary to the DNA strand.
- Each group of three bases on the mRNA strand is called a **codon**.

The base sequence of the mRNA has been determined by the base sequence of the part of the DNA involved. This part of the DNA represents one gene which will eventually lead to the synthesis of one protein.

The mRNA molecule now leaves the nucleus and attaches to a **ribosome**. Ribosomes are small organelles free in the cell cytoplasm or on the membranes of the **rough endoplasmic reticulum**.

2. Transfer RNA (tRNA)

tRNA molecules are smaller than mRNA molecules. They are found in the cytoplasm of cells. There are different forms of tRNA, each of which attaches to a single specific amino acid molecule. Each tRNA molecule has a specific sequence of three exposed bases (a triplet) called an **anticodon**. The synthesis of a protein has a number of stages:

- an mRNA molecule from the nucleus attaches to a ribosome
- a tRNA molecule with a complementary anticodon aligns with the first mRNA codon
- a second tRNA molecule with a complementary anticodon aligns with the second mRNA codon
- the amino acids of adjacent tRNA molecules become linked by peptide bonds and separate from the tRNA
- the mRNA molecule moves across the ribosome and complementary tRNA molecules become aligned with each mRNA codon in turn
- the amino acids from each tRNA continue to add to the growing chain of amino acids
- the amino acid chain eventually becomes a protein molecule
- tRNA molecules that have added their amino acid to the chain move back into the cytoplasm and collect another amino acid of the same type.

The mRNA triplets are called **codons**. The complementary tRNA triplets are the **anti-codons**.

The sequence of the amino acids in the protein has been controlled by the base-pairing between the mRNA and the tRNA molecules. The mRNA base sequence was controlled by the base sequence of the DNA of a single gene on a chromosome. The conversion of mRNA base sequence to protein amino acid sequence is called **translation**.

Summary of nucleic acids and protein synthesis

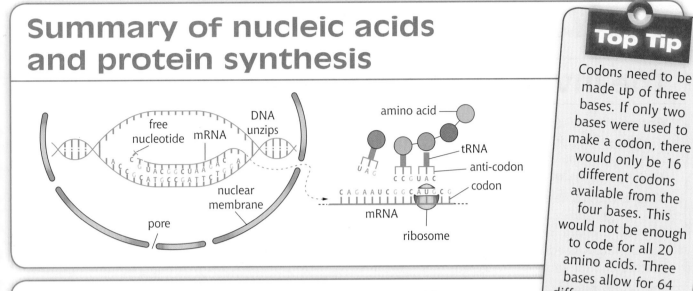

The role of other organelles

Translation of the mRNA base sequence into the amino acid sequence of a protein molecule takes place at the ribosomes. Many of these are free in the cell cytoplasm and the proteins synthesised at these will be used in the cell. Other ribosomes are attached to the membranes of the rough endoplasmic reticulum. These form a transport system for proteins that will be secreted from the cell.

Proteins carried by the rough endoplasmic reticulum become contained in membrane-coated vesicles which pass to another membrane structure called the **Golgi apparatus**. The Golgi apparatus packages and processes proteins ready for secretion from the cell. The proteins are enveloped in membrane material to form a secretory vesicle which moves to and fuses with the plasma membrane of the cell. The protein is released to the outside of the cell.

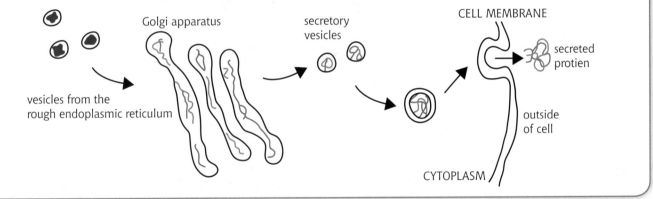

Quick Test 7

1. The table shows the anti-codons of some tRNA molecules and the amino acids they carry. The diagram shows the base sequence of part of an mRNA molecule at a ribosome.

anti-codon	amino acid	anti-codon	amino acid	anti-codon	amino acid	anti-codon	amino acid
AGA	serine	CAC	valine	UCC	arginine	UGU	threonine
AUG	tyrosine	UUU	lysine	GGG	proline	CUA	asparagine
CCC	glycine	GUG	histidine	CGC	alanine	ACG	cysteine

CCC UGC AAA CAC UAC GGG UCU GAU GUG   Starting at the left, what will be the sequence of amino acids in the resulting protein chain?

Cellular defence

The invasion of cells by viruses

Viruses are very small, simple structures that do not show all the features normally associated with living organisms. They do not have a cell structure. They do not feed, carry out respiration or excrete wastes. They can only multiply inside suitable host cells of living organisms. They consist of a protein coat which contains a strand of DNA or RNA.

When a virus comes into contact with a suitable host cell, the viral nucleic acid chain is injected into the cell. The genetic information contained in the viral nucleic acid then takes over the metabolism of the host cell. The viral nucleic acid is replicated many times and viral protein is synthesised. Many new virus particles are formed and released when the host cell breaks down and dies (**lysis**). New host cells are infected and the process is repeated.

Viruses use animals, plants and bacteria as hosts. They are responsible for a range of human diseases including the common cold, influenza, measles, mumps and AIDS.

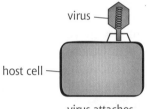

virus —

host cell —

virus attaches
to host cell

viral nucleic acid
is injected into the
host cell and replicates

virus components
produced

virus particles
assembled

lysis of host cell and
the release of viruses

Cellular defence mechanisms in animals

Animals have several defence mechanisms to protect themselves from infection by viruses and by micro-organisms.

The first lines of defence are the physical barriers provided by the skin, stomach acid and the mucus of the air passages. If viruses or bacteria get past these defences and enter the blood, there are two types of white blood cells which will act against them.

The first are white blood cells called **phagocytes**. These have the ability to move in the same way as unicellular amoeba. The phagocytes flow around foreign particles they encounter and engulf them in a vacuole within their cytoplasm.

Top Tip

Phagocytosis is a non-specific response of our immune system since phagocytes will attack a wide range of invading micro-organisms. The production of antibodies is specific to the antigen encountered by the lymphocytes.

This is called **phagocytosis**. Organelles called **lysosomes** in the phagocytes contain powerful enzymes. These are released into the vacuole containing the engulfed particles, which are then digested.

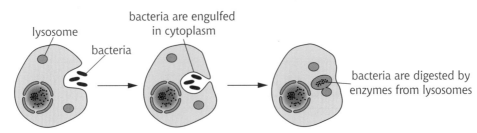

Other white blood cells called **lymphocytes** act in a different way to combat infection by bacteria and viruses. Proteins on the surface of the virus or bacterium are recognised as foreign by the lymphocyte. Such proteins are called **antigens**. The lymphocyte then responds by producing **antibodies** that are **specific** to the antigen. The antibody combines with the antigen to make the antigen harmless.

Phagocytes and lymphocytes are part of the **immune** system of an animal. Sometimes these defences are a problem because they act against any transplanted organs or tissues in the same way as they would against viruses or bacteria. This can cause tissue rejection and make the transplant fail.

Matching the tissue types of the donor and recipient can help reduce the chance of rejection, but normally the immune system of the recipient needs to be made less active. This is done using drugs called **suppressors**. Suppression of the immune system, although necessary, has the disadvantage of making the recipient more vulnerable to infections.

Cellular defence mechanisms in plants

Many plants produce chemicals that are distasteful or toxic to deter herbivores from eating them. Examples of these chemicals include **tannins**, **cyanide** and **nicotine**.

Plants which can produce cyanide are said to be **cyanogenic**. Examples include certain varieties of apple, elderberry and clover.

Some plants produce chemicals such as **resin** and **latex** which seal areas of damage. This produces a barrier which prevents the entry of pathogens such as bacteria, fungi and viruses.

Quick Test 8

1. What feature of viruses provides an argument that they should be considered to be living organisms?
2. What part of an invading virus acts as the antigen which triggers antibody production by a lymphocyte?
3. Ponderosa pine trees produce resin following damage to their bark.
   In an investigation, three individual pine trees were chosen from areas with different population densities. Each tree was damaged by having a hole bored through its bark.
   Measurements of resin production from each hole following this damage are shown in the table.

Population density (trees per hectare)	Volume of resin produced in the first day (cm³)	Duration of resin flow (days)	Total volume of resin produced (cm³)
2	8·3	7·0	29·3
10	0·8	4·8	2·9
50	0·6	4·6	2·8

   (a) (i) How does the population density affect the total volume of resin produced?
       (ii) Calculate the average resin flow per day at a population density of two trees per hectare, **after the first day**.
   (b) Explain how resin production protects trees.

Meiosis and the dihybrid cross 1

Sexual reproduction

Variations are the differences which exist between members of the same species. Some variations are due to the effects of the environment on individual organisms but these have no significance to the species as a whole because they are not inherited.

The most important variations are due to genes inherited from parents through sexual reproduction. Sexual reproduction involves the production of sex cells (**gametes**) by the parents. The gametes from any individual contain countless possible combinations of genetic information. The random nature of fertilisation further increases the variability of the genetic information inherited by an individual. The result is that offspring from sexual reproduction are genetically unique, except for the special case of identical twins.

Meiosis

Gametes are produced by a particular form of cell division in which the cell nucleus divides by a process called **meiosis**.

During cell division for body growth the cell nucleus divides by **mitosis**. DNA replication ensures that both daughter cells contain two sets of chromosomes that are genetically identical to those of the mother cell.

During gamete formation, the nucleus of the **gamete mother cell** divides by meiosis to produce four daughter cells. The gametes each have a single set of chromosomes which are genetically different from each other.

> **Top Tip**
>
> Learn these differences between mitosis and meiosis:
> - Mitosis produces two daughter cells – meiosis produces four.
> - Mitosis produces **diploid** (containing two chromosome sets) daughter cells – meiosis produces **haploid** (containing one chromosome set) daughter cells.
> - Mitosis produces body cells for growth – meiosis produces gametes for reproduction.
> - Mitosis involves one division – meiosis involves two.
> - Mitosis does not involve alignment of **homologous chromosomes** – meiosis does.
> - Mitosis does not involve genetic variation in the daughter cells – meiosis does.

Quick Test 9

1. The table refers to the mass of DNA in certain human body cells.

Cell type	Mass of DNA in cell ($\times 10^{-12}$ g)
liver	6·6
lung	6·6
R	3·3
S	0·0

Which of the following is the most likely identification of cell types R and S?

	R	S
A	ovum	mature red blood cell
B	mature red blood cell	sperm
C	nerve cell	mature red blood cell
D	sperm	kidney tubule cell

2. The letters A–D represent four statements about meiosis.

Letter	Statement	Letter	Statement
A	haploid gametes are produced	C	homologous chromosomes form pairs
B	gamete mother cell is present	D	chromatids separate

Which of the statements are connected with the first meiotic division and which are connected with the second meiotic division?

Division by mitosis
Mother cell before chromosome replication

Division by meiosis
Gamete mother cell before chromosome replication

The mother cell contains two sets of chromosomes (**diploid**). Together these make three homologous pairs of chromosomes. The actual number of chromosomes differs from species to species.

Each chromosome replicates to form a pair of identical chromatids attached by a centromere.

Each chromosome replicates to form a pair of identical chromatids attached by a centromere. Homologous chromosomes become aligned together to form a four-stranded structure.

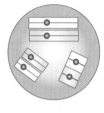

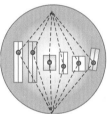

Chromosomes (chromatid pairs) attach by their centromeres to the equator of the spindle.

Pairs of homologous chromosomes (each a pair of chromatids) attach by their centromeres around the equator of the spindle.

This stage is crucial in promoting variation between the gametes.

Contraction of the spindle fibres separates the homologous chromosomes from each other, but not the chromatids of each chromosome.

Each end of the cell receives one chromosome from each pair.

The cytoplasm divides.

This is the end of the first meiotic division.

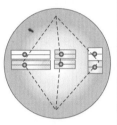

Contraction of the spindle fibres separates the pairs of chromatids. One from each pair passes to opposite ends of the cell. Division of the cytoplasm produces two daughter cells that are genetically identical to the mother cell.

New spindles form at each end of the cell, at right angles to the first.

Chromosomes (still as chromatid pairs) become attached by their centromeres.

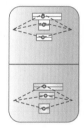

Contraction of the spindle fibres separates the chromatids of each pair.

Division of the cytoplasm produces four daughter cells, the gametes, each with only one set of chromosomes (**haploid**).

This is the end of the second meiotic division.

Meiosis and the dihybrid cross 2

Independent assortment and crossing over

The reduction in chromosome number to one set is an important function of meiosis. Promoting genetic variation in the gametes is equally important. Meiosis does this in a number of ways.

1. Independent assortment

This refers to the way in which the homologous pairs of chromosomes become aligned on the spindle before the first division of meiosis. It means that the way in which one pair of chromosomes becomes aligned about the equator of the spindle is independent of all the other homologous pairs. This applies to all the gametes produced by an individual and it results in many possible chromosome combinations in the gametes.

The diagram below shows the four possible ways in which the chromosomes of the cell from the previous page could become arranged on the spindle prior to the first meiotic division. The resulting combinations of chromosomes in the gametes are also shown.

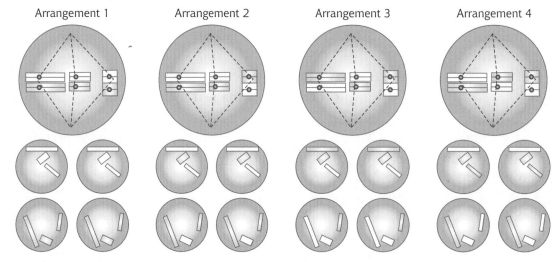

Arrangement 1   Arrangement 2   Arrangement 3   Arrangement 4

Therefore the four possible ways in which the three homologous pairs of chromosomes can align on the spindle produce a total of eight different chromosome combinations in the gametes. Greater numbers of chromosomes in cells will produce a greater range of possible chromosome combinations in the gametes. The formula used to calculate the possible combinations is 2^n, where n = the number of chromosome pairs. In this case n = 3 and so the number of possible chromosome combinations in the gametes is 2^3, or $2 \times 2 \times 2 = 8$.

Human cells have twenty-three pairs of chromosomes and so independent assortment can lead to 2^{23} different chromosome combinations in the gametes. This equals 8 388 608.

2. Crossing over

This process increases the genetic variation of the gametes even further by causing an exchange of sections between one chromatid of a chromosome and a chromatid of its homologous partner. It happens between adjacent chromatids when homologous chromosomes pair up before the first meiotic division.

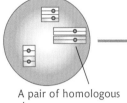

A pair of homologous chromosomes

Adjacent chromatids cross over, forming a chiasma. They break and rejoin after swapping sections.

Two of the chromatids now contain new combinations of genes.

The points at which the adjacent chromatids come together, break and rejoin are called **chiasmata** (singular – **chiasma**).

Crossing over is random. It does not always happen and when it does, it may not be at the same point of the chromatids. It may happen in several places along the same chromatids. The chances of a chiasma forming are greater for long chromosomes than for short ones and greater at points further away from a centromere than close to it.

Together independent assortment and crossing over create new combinations of genetic information contained in the single set of chromosomes of the gametes. This means that every gamete produced by an individual is likely to be unique. When one of these gametes combines with another at fertilisation, new phenotypes can develop in the offspring.

Quick Test 10

1. The diagram shows a cell during meiosis.

   How many of each of the following can be seen in the cell?
   (a) chromosomes 6
   (b) chromatids
   (c) centromeres 6
   (d) homologous pairs of chromosomes 3

2. The diagram shows a stage of meiosis.

   Which of the following diagrams shows the next stage in meiosis?

    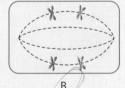 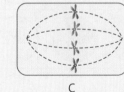 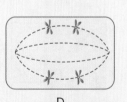

   A   B   C   D

3. The diagram shows a pair of homologous chromosomes prior to the first division of meiosis.

   (a) How many chiasmata are taking place between adjacent chromatids?
   (b) Draw the individual chromatids that would finally end up in the four gametes produced after meiosis is completed.

Meiosis and the dihybrid cross 3

The dihybrid cross phenotype ratios

A **dihybrid cross** is one in which the inheritance of two characteristics is studied. It demonstrates the effect of independent assortment on the number of phenotypes expected. The pattern of inheritance for each characteristic on its own is still the same as monohybrid inheritance, but the combination of the two characteristics produces phenotype ratios that are more complex.

The following diagram shows the inheritance of seed colour and seed shape in pea plants.

In pea plants, yellow seed colour is **dominant** to green seed colour and smooth seed shape is dominant to wrinkled seed shape. The alleles for green seed colour and for wrinkled seed shape are **recessive**. This means that the allele for yellow seed colour will mask the allele for green seed colour if they occur together in an individual. Similarly, the allele for round seed shape will mask that for wrinkled seed shape.

S = the allele for smooth seed shape   Y = the allele for yellow seeds

s = the allele for wrinkled seed shape   y = the allele for green seeds

P genotypes	SSYY		ssyy
P phenotypes	true-breeding plants with smooth yellow seeds	×	true-breeding plants with wrinkled green seeds
P gametes	all SY		all sy
F_1 genotypes		all SsYy	
F_1 phenotypes		all with smooth yellow seeds	
F_1 gametes:	equal numbers of SY Sy sY sy		from each parent because of independent assortment

F_1 plants crossed together

		female gametes			
		SY	Sy	sY	sy
male gametes	SY	SSYY	SSYy	SsYY	SsYy
	Sy	SSYy	SSyy	SsYy	Ssyy
	sY	SsYY	SsYy	ssYY	ssYy
	sy	SsYy	Ssyy	ssYy	ssyy

F_2 phenotypes	smooth yellow seeds	smooth green seeds	wrinkled yellow seeds	wrinkled green seeds
F_2 phenotype ratio	9 :	3 :	3 :	1

Top Tip

Remember, when dealing with dihybrid inheritance, each characteristic must still show the same pattern as with monohybrid inheritance. This means that there must be two alleles represented for each characteristic in the genotype of an individual and one allele represented for each characteristic in each gamete.

There are many dihybrid crosses that could take place involving different genotypes. The other important cross to remember is the cross between a 'double **heterozygous** (contains two different alleles for a characteristic) individual' and a double recessive individual. This is shown below.

Genotypes   SsYy   ×   ssyy

Gametes   SY Sy sY sy   all sy
                   in equal numbers

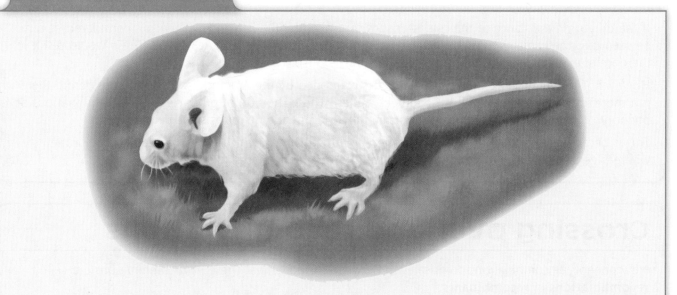

		gametes from double heterozygote			
		SY	Sy	sY	sy
gametes from double recessive	sy	SsYy	Ssyy	ssYy	ssyy

phenotypes   smooth yellow seeds   smooth green seeds   wrinkled yellow seeds   wrinkled green seeds

phenotype ratio   1   :   1   :   1   :   1

This is sometimes referred to as a **test cross**. The significance of this cross will be discussed later.

Quick Test 11

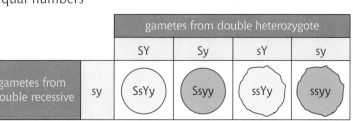

1. In mice, coloured coat (C) is dominant to albino coat (c) and straight hair (S) is dominant to wavy hair (s).
   (a) What would be the genotype of a mouse that was heterozygous for coat colour and had wavy hair?
   (b) A mouse with the genotype ccSs was crossed with a mouse with the genotype CcSs.
       (i) List the genotypes of all the possible gametes produced by each mouse.
       (ii) Work out the phenotype ratio of the offspring of this cross.

2. In horses, coat colour is determined by two genes. The allele for black coat (B) is dominant to the allele for chestnut coat (b). The allele for grey coat (G) is dominant to the allele for non-grey coat (g).
   Horses with the allele G are always grey.
   A male with the genotype GgBb was crossed with a female with the genotype ggBb.
   (a) State the phenotype for each parent.
   (b) Work out the genotypes of all the possible gametes from each parent.
   (c) Work out the genotypes of the possible offspring from the cross.
   (d) Give the expected ratio of Grey : Black : Chestnut offspring from the cross.

Linkage & crossing over

Linked genes

The typical ratios obtained from dihybrid inheritance assume that the genes controlling the two characteristics are carried on different chromosomes. This allows independent assortment to produce all possible combinations of the genes in the gametes.

Each chromosome carries genes for many different characteristics, and the genes that are part of the same chromosome are said to be **linked**. Such genes do not show normal dihybrid phenotype ratios because independent assortment only applies if two or more different chromosomes are involved.

Consider the inheritance of characteristics controlled by the genes A/a, B/b and C/c carried on different chromosomes of an organism as shown on the left.

The gametes from this organism could contain the following possible combinations of chromosomes.

If the dihybrid inheritance of the characteristics controlled by the A/a and C/c genes is considered, it can be seen that the gametes show the full range of possible genotypes: AC Ac aC ac. These would result in the normal expected dihybrid phenotype ratios in the offspring.

However, if the inheritance of the characteristics controlled by the A/a and B/b genes is considered, there is a more limited range of possible genotypes: AB ab. These should not produce the new combinations of phenotypes in the offspring and so the normal dihybrid phenotype ratios should not be seen.

This is because genes A/a and C/c are on different chromosomes, which show independent assortment, whereas genes A/a and B/b are on the same chromosome and so are linked.

Crossing over and recombinations

New phenotype combinations do arise even between linked genes. These new combinations are called **recombinations** or **recombinants**.

Recombinants are produced because of the process of crossing over, described earlier.

Quick Test 12

1. The recombination frequency obtained in a genetic cross may be used as a source of information concerning which of the following:
   A   genotypes of the recombinant offspring
   B   diploid number of the species
   C   fertility of the species
   D   position of gene loci?

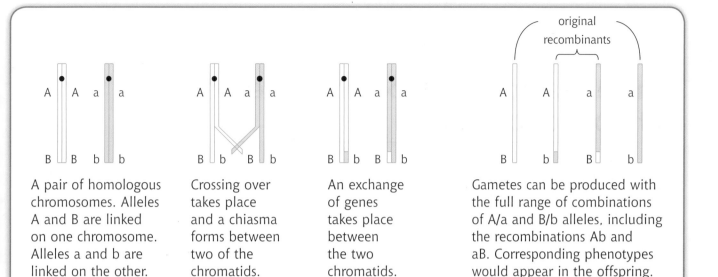

original
recombinants

A pair of homologous chromosomes. Alleles A and B are linked on one chromosome. Alleles a and b are linked on the other.

Crossing over takes place and a chiasma forms between two of the chromatids.

An exchange of genes takes place between the two chromatids.

Gametes can be produced with the full range of combinations of A/a and B/b alleles, including the recombinations Ab and aB. Corresponding phenotypes would appear in the offspring.

Chromosome mapping

Recombinations of linked genes are more likely to form between genes that are far apart on the chromosome than if they are close together. Therefore the frequency of recombination is used as a measure of how close together linked genes are. This is an important tool in **chromosome mapping**, i.e. building up a picture of the arrangement of all the genes on a chromosome (**gene loci**).

Example – Genes P, Q and R linked.

Recombination frequencies from test crosses are:

PpQq × ppqq = 18%
PpRr × pprr = 15%
QqRr × qqrr = 3%

The relative positions of the genes can now be worked out.

P and Q are a distance of 18 units apart.

P and R are slightly closer together, with a distance of 15 units.

Q and R are close together at a distance of 3 units and R must be between P and Q because P and R are closer than P and Q.

2. The following table shows the recombination frequency of four linked genes obtained from test crosses in the fruit fly *Drosophila*.

Linked genes used in test cross	Recombination frequency (%)
presence or absence of bristles (A) × straight or curved wing (B)	25
thick or thin leg (C) × presence or absence of bristles (A)	4
presence or absence of bristles (A) × long or vestigial wing (D)	16
straight or curved wing (B) × thick or thin leg (C)	21
thick or thin leg (C) × long or vestigial wing (D)	12

(a) Draw a chromosome to show the relative positions of genes A, B, C and D.
(b) What would be the recombination frequency obtained in a test cross involving genes B and D?

Sex linkage

Inheritance of sex and the sex chromosomes

The inheritance of sex is different from the inheritance of other characteristics. The sex of an individual is controlled by the possession of a complete pair of chromosomes and not by individual genes. The sex chromosomes are known as **X** and **Y chromosomes**.

In humans, the inheritance of two X chromosomes produces a female and the inheritance of an X and a Y chromosome produces a male. The egg cells of a female must contain a single X chromosome, whereas the sperm of a male can contain either a single X or a single Y chromosome. Therefore, sex is determined by the sperm which fertilises an egg. If the sperm contains an X chromosome, the resulting XX zygote will develop into a female. If the sperm contains a Y chromosome, the XY zygote will develop into a male.

Only X chromosomes carry genes for other characteristics. Y chromosomes are smaller than X chromosomes and so carry fewer genes, all associated with sexual development. This means that most genes found on X chromosomes are not represented on Y chromosomes.

human X chromosome  human Y chromosome

Sex-linked inheritance

When following the inheritance of sex-linked characteristics, a different system is used because the sex chromosomes must be represented, as well as the alleles for the characteristic.

For example, part of our ability to see colour is controlled by a gene that is present on X chromosomes but not on Y chromosomes. The gene has two alleles. The normal dominant allele (N) gives normal colour vision but the recessive allele (n) can cause red–green colour blindness.

A man with normal colour vision is represented as X^NY. A woman who is heterozygous is represented as X^NX^n.

If this couple produced a child, the inheritance of the sex chromosomes and colour vision alleles can be followed as shown.

Parent genotypes	X^NX^n		$\times$		X^NY	
Parent phenotypes	female with normal vision (note that she is heterozygous and carries a recessive allele)				male with normal vision	
Gametes	X^N	X^n		X^N		Y
Children's genotypes	X^NX^N	X^NX^n		X^NY		X^nY
Children's phenotypes	female normal vision	female normal vision (carrier)		male normal vision		male red-green colour blindness

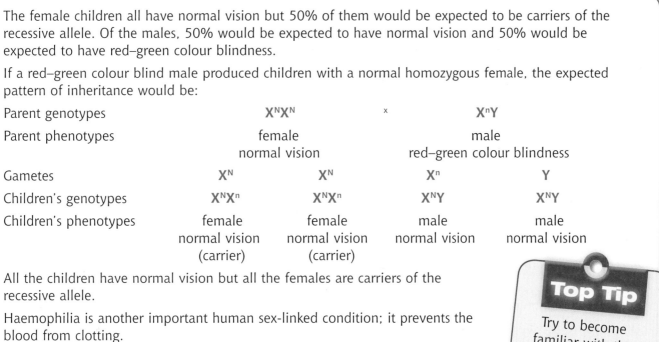

The female children all have normal vision but 50% of them would be expected to be carriers of the recessive allele. Of the males, 50% would be expected to have normal vision and 50% would be expected to have red–green colour blindness.

If a red–green colour blind male produced children with a normal homozygous female, the expected pattern of inheritance would be:

Parent genotypes	$X^N X^N$	x		$X^n Y$
Parent phenotypes	female			male
	normal vision			red–green colour blindness
Gametes	X^N	X^N	X^n	Y
Children's genotypes	$X^N X^n$	$X^N X^n$	$X^N Y$	$X^N Y$
Children's phenotypes	female	female	male	male
	normal vision	normal vision	normal vision	normal vision
	(carrier)	(carrier)		

All the children have normal vision but all the females are carriers of the recessive allele.

Haemophilia is another important human sex-linked condition; it prevents the blood from clotting.

Sex-linked inheritance often shows the following features:

- The recessive condition appears predominantly in males because there is a greater chance of a male receiving one recessive allele than of a female receiving two.
- The condition often skips a generation because the male children of an affected male usually do not show the condition but the unaffected female children are carriers of it.

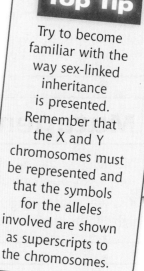

Top Tip

Try to become familiar with the way sex-linked inheritance is presented. Remember that the X and Y chromosomes must be represented and that the symbols for the alleles involved are shown as superscripts to the chromosomes.

Quick Test 13

1. The symbol H represents the allele for normal blood clotting and the symbol h represents the haemophilic allele.
   Give the genotypes for the following people:
   (a) a normal male
   (b) a haemophilic male
   (c) a homozygous normal female
   (d) a carrier female
2. In *Drosophila* eye colour is sex-linked. The gene for red eyes (R) is dominant to the gene for white eyes (r).
   Determine the possible genotype and phenotype ratios expected from a cross between:
   (a) a heterozygous female and a red-eyed male
   (b) a heterozygous female and a white-eyed male

Mutation 1

The nature of mutations

Independent assortment and crossing over have both been mentioned as contributing to genetic variability. Both these mechanisms produce new combinations of existing genetic information and can lead to new phenotypes appearing in a population. However, they do not produce new genetic information. **Mutation** is the only way in which entirely new genetic information can arise naturally.

Mutations are caused by errors during cell division. Errors happening during meiosis can be particularly significant because these may become part of the genotype of a new individual. If they do so, they may become established in the whole population.

Mutations are random events and take place relatively infrequently. It has been estimated that in every one million gametes between 1 and 30 of them will contain a mutation.

Mutations tend to be lethal because any mistake in the genetic instructions will probably result in some aspect of the organism not functioning properly. The gamete itself or the resulting embryo may fail to develop.

On very rare occasions, a mutation may produce an improvement in the organism inheriting it. This is the source of variations which are most important to the evolutionary development of organisms.

Mutagenic agents

Although specific mutations cannot be made to happen, there are some factors that are known to increase the rate at which mutations occur. Such factors are referred to as **mutagenic agents** or **mutagens**.

Known mutagenic agents include various forms of radiation such as X-rays, gamma rays and ultraviolet light. Some chemicals such as colchicine and mustard gas are also known to cause mutations.

Mutations involving changes in chromosome number

1. Non-disjunction

During the first division of meiosis, pairs of homologous chromosomes are arranged together and then separated, with one of the pair going to one end of the cell and the other of the pair going to the other end. Sometimes this does not happen because of a failure of the spindle and both chromosomes of the pair move to the same end of the cell. This is called non-disjunction. If meiosis then continues normally, it will result in gametes with one chromosome missing and an equal number of gametes with one chromosome extra. If a gamete with this kind of mutation undergoes fertilisation with a normal gamete then the zygote will have one extra chromosome or have one chromosome missing. This sort of error usually results in the failure of the embryo to develop but there are a number of human conditions caused by non-disjunction. Examples are:

* Down's syndrome – caused by an extra chromosome number 21.
* Klinefelter's syndrome – caused by an extra X chromosome giving an XXY complement of sex chromosomes.
* Turner's syndrome – caused by the loss of an X chromosome to leave just a single X chromosome.

Mutations such as these can be detected before birth by amniocentesis or chorionic villi sampling.

Changes to the chromosome number usually reduce the fertility of an individual, because some chromosomes are unable to form homologous pairs during meiosis.

2. Polyploidy

In plants, **total non-disjunction** can happen. This means that none of the homologous chromosomes separate during the first division of meiosis, thus producing gametes with two full sets of chromosomes, the same as the normal cells of the plant.

Fertilisation involving such gametes can produce offspring with multiple sets of chromosomes (**polyploid**). These offspring may be fertile because pairing of homologous chromosomes can still take place during meiosis. Polyploid plants often show increased vigour, resulting in increased crop yields and increased resistance to disease. This means that polyploidy has been important in the development of many crop species. Polyploidy has also enabled successful interbreeding of closely related species to take place.

Top Tip

Make yourself familiar with the meaning of the term **ploidy** and similar words.

Ploidy refers to the number of complete sets of chromosomes in a cell. This number is sometimes represented as 'n'.

Normal body cells have two sets of chromosomes and are diploid, with a chromosome number of 2n.

Gametes have one set of chromosomes and are haploid, with a chromosome number of n.

Polyploid cells or organisms possess one or more sets of chromosomes in addition to the normal diploid number, and may have chromosome numbers of 3n, 4n or even more.

Quick Test 14

1. What does polyploidy in plants result from?
   A total spindle failure during meiosis
   B hybridisation between varieties of the same species
   C homologous chromosomes binding at chiasmata
   D the failure of linked genes to separate
2. The diagram shows stages in meiosis during which a mutation occurred, and the effect of the mutation on the gametes produced.

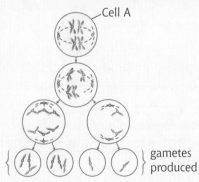

Cell A

gametes produced

   (a) What name is given to cells such as A which undergo meiosis?
   (b) Cell A contains two pairs of homologous chromosomes.
        Apart from size and shape, state one similarity between homologous chromosomes.
   (c) This mutation has resulted in changes to the chromosome numbers in the gametes.
        Name this type of mutation.
   (d) State whether the mutation has occurred in the first or second meiotic division and justify your choice.
   (e) State the expected haploid number of chromosomes in the gametes produced if this mutation **had not occurred**.

Mutation 2

Mutations involving changes to the structure of a chromosome

During meiosis, the mechanism involved in crossing over can cause errors by breaking and rejoining sections of chromosomes wrongly. Several types of these mutations have been identified.

- **Deletion** – a chromosome breaks in two places and rejoins with a section being missed out. This is usually lethal, since genes have been lost.
- **Inversion** – a chromosome breaks in two places and rejoins with a section the wrong way round, producing a new sequence of genes. The effect of this may be harmful or beneficial depending on the new gene sequence produced.
- **Translocation** – a chromosome breaks and the separated section is joined to a different chromosome. This is usually lethal.
- **Duplication** – a section of a chromosome is copied twice during chromosome replication. This may be harmless as there is no loss of genes.

In all of these cases, sections of chromosomes containing a number of genes are lost or wrongly placed. The effects vary but normally any loss of genes will be lethal.

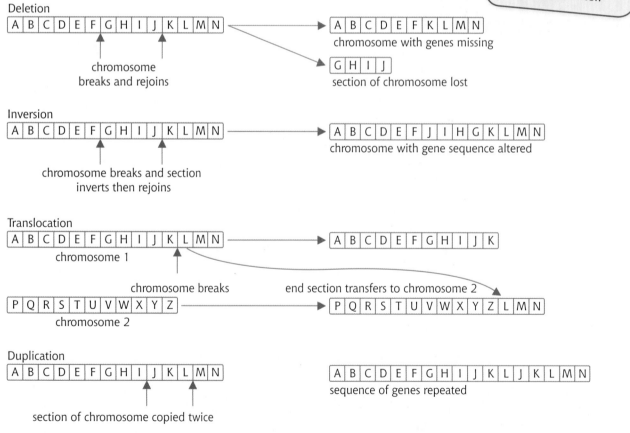

Deletion

chromosome breaks and rejoins

chromosome with genes missing

section of chromosome lost

Inversion

chromosome breaks and section inverts then rejoins

chromosome with gene sequence altered

Translocation

chromosome 1

chromosome breaks

chromosome 2

end section transfers to chromosome 2

Duplication

section of chromosome copied twice

sequence of genes repeated

Changes in chromosome structure

Cri-Du-Chat Syndrome is caused by a deletion mutation affecting one of the number 5 pair of chromosomes. People affected suffer from heart defects, muscular or skeletal problems, hearing or sight problems, or poor muscle tone. When they grow older they experience difficulty walking and talking.

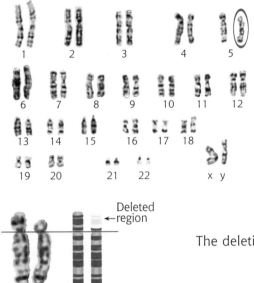

Human karyotype showing a deletion mutation from one of the number 5 pair of chromosomes, resulting in Cri-Du-Chat Syndrome.

The deletion is more clearly seen in the adjacent photograph and diagram.

Quick Test 15

1. The diagram shows two chromosomes and their appearance after a mutation has occurred.

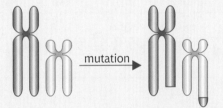

   (a) Name this type of mutation.
   (b) Name a mutagenic agent which could have caused this mutation.

2. Duchenne muscular dystrophy (DMD) is a recessive sex-linked condition in humans that affects muscular function.
   The diagram shows an X-chromosome from an unaffected individual and one from an individual with DMD.

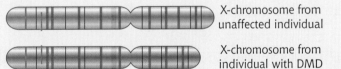

   X-chromosome from unaffected individual

   X-chromosome from individual with DMD

   (a) Using information from the diagram, name the type of chromosome mutation responsible for DMD.
   (b) On the diagram of the chromosome of the unaffected individual, identify the likely location of the gene involved in DMD.
   (c) Males are more likely to be affected by DMD than females.
       Explain why.
   (d) A person with DMD has an altered phenotype compared with an unaffected individual.
       Explain how an inherited chromosome mutation such as DMD may result in an altered phenotype.

Mutation 3

Mutations involving changes to DNA bases

These errors happen during DNA replication when chromosomes are being duplicated to form two identical chromatids. They produce changes to individual genes rather than the overall structure of a chromosome. There are several types of these mistakes.

- **Substitution** – an incorrect nucleotide is placed in the new DNA chain in place of the correct one. This will affect one triplet of bases and so will result in one incorrect amino acid being inserted into a protein during its synthesis. This type of error can have variable effects depending on the role of the protein and how much its function is impaired by the error.
- **Inversion** – two or more nucleotides are positioned in the new DNA chain the wrong way round. This will affect one or more triplets of bases and so one or more incorrect amino acids will be inserted into a protein chain during its synthesis. The effects will vary depending on how big a change to the original base sequence results.
- **Deletion** – one nucleotide is missed from the new DNA chain. This has the effect of moving every nucleotide from that point one place along and so every base triplet from that point will be different. Every amino acid from the corresponding point of the protein chain will be different and so the effect can be very severe.
- **Insertion** – one extra nucleotide is positioned in the new DNA chain. Every nucleotide from that point will be moved along and so every triplet in the chain will be different and every amino acid from the corresponding point of the resulting protein chain will be different. Again, the effects can be very severe.

Part of original DNA chain

DNA base sequence	CCG	GTG	TCA	TGT	GGT	AAG
mRNA codons	GGC	CAC	AGU	ACA	CCA	UUC
resulting amino acid sequence	glycine	histidine	serine	threonine	proline	phenylalanine

Effect of substitution

A replaces T here		↓				
DNA base sequence	CCG	GAG	TCA	TGT	GGT	AAG
mRNA codons	GGC	CUC	AGU	ACA	CCA	UUC
resulting amino acid sequence	glycine	leucine	serine	threonine	proline	phenylalanine

Effect of inversion

G and T reversed here		↓				
DNA base sequence	CCG	GGT	TCA	TGT	GGT	AAG
mRNA codons	GGC	CCA	AGU	ACA	CCA	UUC
resulting amino acid sequence	glycine	proline	serine	threonine	proline	phenylalanine

Top Tip

These types of mutation are of particular importance because they are the only mechanism in which new genetic information can be created. They are mistakes and therefore very unlikely to produce changes that provide any advantage to an individual inheriting them. However, over the course of time beneficial mutations have occurred which have allowed the evolution of the wide variety of life present today.

Effect of deletion

G lost from original chain here		↓		all bases moved one place to the left		
DNA base sequence	CCG	TGT	CAT	GTG	GTA	AG
mRNA codons	GGC	ACA	GUA	CAC	CAU	UC
resulting amino acid sequence	glycine	cysteine	valine	histidine	histidine	

Effect of insertion

additional G added here		↓		all bases moved one place to the right			
DNA base sequence	CCG	GGT	GTC	ATG	TGG	TAA	G
mRNA codons	GGC	CAC	AGU	ACA	CCA	UUC	
resulting amino acid sequence	glycine	proline	glutamine	tyrosine	threonine	isoleucine	

Quick Test 16

1. The base sequence of a short piece of DNA is shown below.
    A G C T T A C G
    During replication, an inversion mutation occurred on the complementary strand synthesised on this piece of DNA.
    Which of the following is the mutated complementary strand?
    A T C G A A T G A
    B A G C T T A G C
    C T C G A A T C G
    D T C G A A T G C
2. Name the two types of gene mutation that are likely to have the most severe consequences.
    Explain why this is the case.
3. The diagram shows the sequence of bases on part of a DNA strand.
    A C C G A T A C G T G A A
    The following show the results of two different gene mutations on the strand.
    (a) A C C G A T C A G T G A A
    (b) A C C G A T A G G T G A A
    Name the type of gene mutation in each case.

Natural selection 1

The survival of those organisms best suited to their environment

In 1859 Charles Darwin published a controversial book entitled 'On the Origin of Species by means of Natural Selection'. Today, Darwin's theory of **natural selection** is widely accepted as correct. His explanation of how all living organisms came to exist in their present form was based on a wide range of evidence. He collected data from studies of geology, fossils, embryology, anatomy, the geographical distribution of organisms and the selective breeding of domesticated plants and animals.

The key points of Darwin's theory are:

- Organisms tend to produce more offspring than the environment can support.
- Individuals in a population of plants or animals are not identical but show variations from each other.
- There is competition for resources between individuals in a population.
- Some individuals have a better chance of survival because of the favourable variations they possess.
- These individuals will be more likely to reproduce and pass these characteristics to their offspring.
- The favourable characteristics will gradually increase in the population from generation to generation.
- The characteristics of the population as a whole will slowly change.

This is a continuing process because new variations are always appearing.

The species

A **species** is usually defined as a group of organisms which are able to interbreed and produce fertile offspring.

This means that within a species there is always the possibility that any of the genes present in the population will be passed down to following generations. Even though the species as a whole is changing because of natural selection, it remains a single species as long as its members can successfully interbreed.

Isolating mechanisms and speciation

Accumulated variations will eventually make the species so different from its ancestral form that it will be considered to be a different species. In other words, it will have evolved.

The gradual change of one species into another does not explain increases in the number of species that have happened during the evolution of life on earth. For this to happen, **speciation** must take place. This is when one species becomes two or more species. This can occur when a population of organisms is separated into two or more breeding sub-populations by **isolating mechanisms** which act as barriers to gene exchange between the two groups.

Variations will continue to arise within each group. These variations may be different in the two groups. The effects of natural selection will be different due to different environmental conditions facing each group.

Over a long time, changes will accumulate within each group to the extent that successful interbreeding can not take place between members of different groups, even if the isolating barriers were removed. The different groups would then be considered to be different species.

Isolating barriers can be of different types:

- **Geographical** – these are physical barriers such as rivers, seas, mountains and deserts which can gradually develop and separate a population into isolated groups or sub-populations.
- **Ecological** – these are changes in conditions such as temperature, pH or water availability which can create regions unsuitable to a population and then separate it into sub-populations.

- **Reproductive** – these are factors which prevent successful reproduction. They develop during periods when sub-populations are isolated by a physical barrier and then prevent reproduction when the barrier is removed. Examples of reproductive barriers are different courtship behaviour, failure of pollination mechanisms and differences in breeding or flowering times.

Adaptive radiation

As a population grows, competition between the individuals increases. Variations which appear may allow some individuals to exploit alternative resources. Such variations would be beneficial because these individuals would face less competition. This may lead to the evolution of a distinct group from within the population, and eventually a new species. The evolution of a single species into several different species that are adapted to different ecological **niches** is called **adaptive radiation**.

Good examples of adaptive radiation can be seen on isolated volcanic islands. These have emerged from the oceans with no living organisms present. Accidental colonisation of these islands may introduce individuals of species from the nearest mainland. If their numbers increase then adaptive radiation can lead to the evolution of unique species, each adapted to make use of unexploited resources.

The most famous examples of this are the finches that Charles Darwin studied on the Galapagos Islands. He found many different unique species of finches which had all evolved from a single mainland species.

> **Top Tip**
>
> Remember, evolution is not deliberate. A species does not adapt itself to its environment on purpose. It depends on accidental mutations to produce variations which give some individuals a slight advantage over others. Natural selection gives these individuals a greater chance of survival.

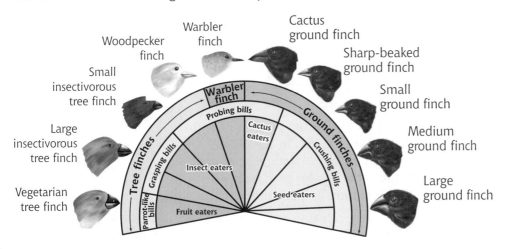

Quick Test 17

1. The diagram shows how an isolating mechanism can divide a population of one species into two sub-populations and then act as a barrier to prevent gene exchange between them.

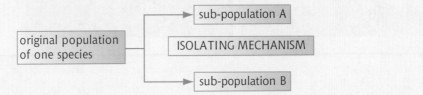

   (a) Name one type of isolation that could prevent gene exchange between sub-populations A and B.
   (b) Over a long period of time, the gene pools of sub-populations A and B become different from each other.
       (i) Explain how mutation and natural selection account for the differences.
       (ii) Eventually sub-populations A and B may become two different species. What evidence would confirm that this had happened?

Natural selection 2

High-speed evolution

One problem with Darwin's theory of evolution is that the timescales involved are so great that the changes cannot be observed. However, there are some examples of evolution which demonstrate Darwin's ideas but which take place in a timescale short enough to be observed or recorded.

1. Antibiotic-resistant bacteria

Mutations which give resistance to an antibiotic arise randomly in populations of bacteria. Such resistance is an advantage only if the population comes into contact with the antibiotic. If this happens, bacteria with the resistance will survive and those without will be killed. The survivors will pass on their resistance to their offspring, giving rise to a population of bacteria that are all resistant to the antibiotic.

Further mutations can take place which produce resistance to higher and higher doses of the antibiotic. A different antibiotic would be needed to treat diseases caused by the bacteria. Resistance to the new antibiotic will eventually develop in the same way.

The indiscriminate use of antibiotics contributes to the problem of resistant bacteria and makes the constant development of new antibiotics a necessity.

2. Peppered moths

The peppered moth is native to Britain. During the daytime it rests on trees, where it may be eaten by birds. Its light grey colour gives it some protection by camouflaging it against the tree bark.

Random mutations occasionally produce dark-coloured **melanic** forms of the moth. These are more easily seen and eaten. Natural selection therefore works against them and they never form a significant proportion of the population.

During the Industrial Revolution in the mid 1800s, increased pollution caused the darkening of tree trunks close to many industrial towns. In these areas the melanic forms of the moth were now better camouflaged. Natural selection favoured them and the normal (light) form suffered greater predation. The melanic form made up the majority of the population in many industrial areas.

In recent years, pollution due to soot deposits has decreased and so the melanic forms are losing their selective advantage. Their numbers are decreasing because the light form of the moth now has the selective advantage.

Top Tip

The peppered moth does not demonstrate the continuing evolution of a species into a new species or into two different species. However, it does show the effect of natural selection and demonstrates how particular variations can be favoured over other variations as a result of environmental conditions.

The conservation of species

As the human population increases, greater demands for resources are resulting in large-scale destruction of natural ecosystems. This threatens the survival of many plant and animal species. Some are well known, such as the giant panda, the black rhinoceros and the Siberian tiger. However, there are undoubtedly many other examples that have become extinct or will do so as human exploitation of the earth's resources continues.

Various conservation measures have been introduced to protect vulnerable species. These include the creation of wildlife reserves and captive breeding programmes, and the storage of gametes and seeds in cell banks. Such measures aim to protect genetic diversity within species. As the numbers of a species decreases, inbreeding increases. This makes it more likely that individuals will suffer from the effects of recessive genes. The genetic material present in conserved individuals, gametes and seeds may be important to the continuing health of their species and also to humans as potential foods, medicines and raw materials.

Quick Test 18

1. Which of the following statements is true about members of the same species?
   A they are separated by isolating barriers
   B they have the same number of chromosomes
   C they cannot interbreed
   D they have different ancestral species from each other
2. Arrange the following events into the correct sequence according to Darwin's theory of evolution.
   A Competition exists between individuals in a population.
   B Variation exists between individuals in a population.
   C The best-adapted individuals reproduce.
   D The best-adapted individuals survive.
   E A new species emerges.
3. Tetracycline is an antibiotic which kills bacteria.
   Strains of bacteria which are resistant to tetracycline have evolved.
   The information below shows some stages in the evolution of tetracycline resistance in bacteria.

   Stage 1 Original population of bacteria.

   Stage 2 A mutant bacterium arose in the population. The mutant had an abnormal membrane protein which prevented tetracycline entering the cell.

   Stage 3 The population of bacteria was exposed to tetracycline.

   Stage 4 Natural selection led to the evolution of a resistant strain of bacteria.

   (a) Explain how a gene mutation would lead to the production of the abnormal membrane protein described in stage 2.
   (b) Explain how tetracycline acts as an agent for natural selection and how this leads to the evolution of a resistant population of bacteria.
4. The melanic variety of the peppered moth became common in industrial areas of Britain following the increase in the production of soot during the industrial revolution.
   Was the increase in the melanic variety due to:
   A melanic moths migrating to areas which gave the best camouflage
   B a change in selection pressure
   C an increase in the mutation rate
   D a change in the prey species taken by birds?
5. Explain why it is considered important to preserve historic breeds of sheep that are no longer kept for commercial reasons.

Artificial selection

Selective breeding

The mechanism involved in Darwin's theory of natural selection can be seen in the development of domesticated varieties of plants and animals by selective breeding. The difference is that in artificial selection, humans provide the selection of which individuals breed and which don't. **Selective breeding** can be more severe than natural selection and the changes which result can take place much faster.

Artificial selection usually involves inbreeding in an attempt to concentrate the genes responsible for the desired features. This can cause problems due to the increased chance of recessive alleles coming together. Hybridisation is sometimes used to reduce this problem. It involves breeding genetically different individuals of the same species and it can result in hybrid vigour in which the offspring are stronger and more fertile than the parents. Hybridisation is also used in an attempt to combine desirable features from two individuals into a single hybrid offspring.

Genetic engineering

Genetic engineering, or genetic modification, involves the transfer of genes from one organism to another. It confers new properties to the receiving organism, enabling it to produce proteins it had been unable to do previously. Bacteria are the usual receiving organisms and they have been genetically modified to produce a range of useful materials. These include human insulin for the treatment of diabetes, human growth hormone for the treatment of growth disorders and digestive enzymes for inclusion in biological detergents.

It is important to be able to locate the required genes on the chromosomes of the donor species. This can be done using **gene probes**. The stages involved in this are:

- establishing the sequence of the amino acids on part of the desired protein product
- using the amino acid sequence to work out the DNA base sequence for these amino acids
- synthesising a nucleic acid chain which is complementary to the DNA base sequence, using nucleotides that carry radioactive markers. This is the gene probe.
- isolating the DNA containing the required gene from the donor organism and cutting it into single-stranded fragments using enzymes
- adding the gene probe to the DNA fragments
- the gene probe will combine with complementary DNA fragments. These will contain the required gene and will be easily identified and isolated because of the radioactive labels on the gene probe.

The manipulation of the nucleic acids is done using enzymes of different types:

- **Endonuclease** enzymes cut DNA chains at positions where there is a particular sequence of bases. Different endonuclease enzymes cut the chains at positions with different base sequences.

- **Ligase** enzymes join DNA chains together. They are used to add the new gene into the chromosomal material of the bacteria.

Chromosome banding patterns can also be used to identify the sites of particular genes. When chromosomes are stained they may show bands that are characteristic for that chromosome. This feature can be used to help match up homologous pairs when examining chromosomes. It can also help establish the location of a particular gene. For example, if an organism shows a feature which results from the loss of a gene by a deletion mutation, the relevant chromosome may show a change to its banding pattern. The position of the change to the pattern is likely to be the position where the deleted gene would normally be found.

Somatic fusion

Different species cannot interbreed and produce fertile offspring. Somatic fusion can be used to overcome sexual incompatibility between two different plant species. New species of plant have been successfully created. The stages involved are:

- removal of the cell walls from the required cells of two plant species using cellulase enzyme. This creates structures called **protoplasts** (plant cells without cell walls).
- treating the protoplasts with chemicals or an electric current to make the membranes of the two cells fuse together
- the nuclei of the two cells fuse to form a nucleus with the diploid chromosome number of both cells
- the combined cell divides repeatedly by mitosis to form a mass of cells called a **callus**
- the callus is treated with plant growth substances and it develops into a new polyploid plant showing characteristics of both parent species.

Top Tip

Remember, each of these techniques also has disadvantages:

- Selective breeding – unforeseen variations still appear and so results are not guaranteed. It takes several generations before changes are likely to be seen.
- Genetic engineering – risk of spread of genes from modified organisms into wild populations, with unknown results.
- Somatic fusion – ethical issues concerning the creation of hybrid species, especially when the technique is applied to animal species.

Quick Test 19

1. Which of the following is the result of artificial selection?
   A Increases in the proportion of the melanic form of the peppered moth in industrial areas.
   B Bacteria becoming resistant to specific antibiotics.
   C Rabbits becoming resistant to the deliberately introduced disease myxomatosis.
   D Development of hill sheep breeds able to cope with harsh conditions.
2. The list below contains terms related to genetic engineering and somatic fusion.

   Terms   cellulase
                gene probe
                ligase
                plasmid
                protoplast
                restriction endonuclease

   Match each of the following descriptions to the correct term from the list.

   Description Contains bacterial genes
                Cuts DNA into fragments
                Locates specific genes
                Removes plant cell walls
3. Describe the problem in plant breeding that is overcome by somatic fusion.

Maintaining a water balance in animals

Osmoregulation in freshwater fish and saltwater bony fish

Bony fish have body fluids that are either hypertonic or hypotonic to their surroundings.

Freshwater fish are hypertonic to the surrounding freshwater. Saltwater bony fish are hypotonic to the surrounding sea water. Therefore both types of fish face osmotic problems.

The gills of fish are adapted to allow gas exchange between the fish's blood and the surrounding water. They also provide an ideal surface for water gain or water loss by osmosis, and for the gain or loss of salts by diffusion.

The problems of both types of fish and the solutions to the problems are summarised in the following table.

Type of fish	Problem	Solution	Kidney adaptation
Freshwater fish	Constant gain of water by osmosis causing dilution of body fluids	Production of large volumes of dilute urine	Many large glomeruli create a high filtration rate
	Problem	**Solution**	
	Loss of salts by diffusion from fish to water	Special chloride secretory cells in the gills actively absorb salts from the surrounding water against the concentration gradient.	
Saltwater bony fish	Constant loss of water by osmosis causing concentration of body fluids	1. Production of small volumes of concentrated urine 2. Drink sea water	Few small glomeruli reduce filtration rate
	Problem	**Solution**	
	Intake of salts by diffusion from water to fish	Special chloride secretory cell in the gills actively excrete salts to the surrounding water against the concentration gradient.	

The action of the **chloride secretory cells** in moving the salts against the concentration gradient is an example of **active transport** and requires energy expenditure by the cells.

Migratory fish

Some species of fish move between freshwater and saltwater as part of their life cycles.

The Atlantic salmon lays its eggs in European rivers and the young fish live in the fresh water for several years. They then move downstream, spend some time in the river estuary, and then migrate to the seas near Canada.

After a number of years they swim back to the river they hatched in. Again they spend some time in the estuary before swimming upriver to breed.

Therefore, the salmon must adapt from freshwater to saltwater and then back again. The time spent in the estuaries allows acclimatisation from one environment to the other. In this time, changes in hormone production alter the filtration rate in the kidney glomeruli and the direction of salt transport by the chloride secretory cells.

Desert mammals

Top Tip

Revise Standard Grade work on the functioning of the kidneys so that you can apply it to these examples of adaptations related to particular environments.

Animals living in very arid areas need to be adapted to conserve water.

A good example is the Desert Rat or Gerbil. All members of this family show a variety of adaptations which help them to survive. The adaptations are both **physiological** and **behavioural**.

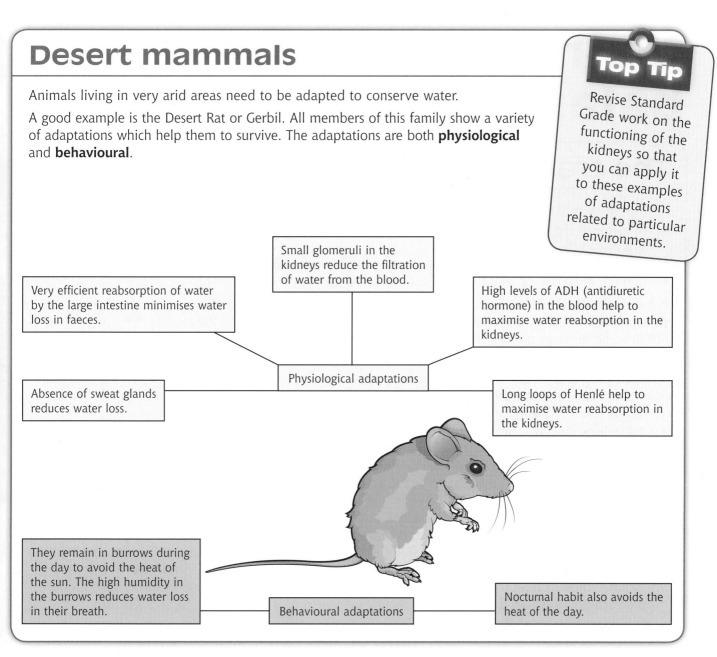

Small glomeruli in the kidneys reduce the filtration of water from the blood.

Very efficient reabsorption of water by the large intestine minimises water loss in faeces.

High levels of ADH (antidiuretic hormone) in the blood help to maximise water reabsorption in the kidneys.

Physiological adaptations

Absence of sweat glands reduces water loss.

Long loops of Henlé help to maximise water reabsorption in the kidneys.

They remain in burrows during the day to avoid the heat of the sun. The high humidity in the burrows reduces water loss in their breath.

Behavioural adaptations

Nocturnal habit also avoids the heat of the day.

Quick Test 20

1. Say whether each of the following statements applies to freshwater fish or to saltwater bony fish.

small kidney glomeruli	produce large volumes of urine	chloride secretory cells excrete salts
large kidney glomeruli	produce small volumes of urine	chloride secretory cells absorb salts
many kidney glomeruli	produce concentrated urine	blood hypotonic to surroundings
few kidney glomeruli	produce dilute urine	blood hypertonic to surroundings

2. In a desert mammal, which of the following is a physiological adaptation which helps to conserve water?
   A nocturnal foraging
   B breathing humid air in a burrow
   C having few sweat glands
   D remaining underground by day

3. Describe the problems faced by a saltwater bony fish in maintaining a water balance and the adaptations they possess which allow them to overcome these problems.

Maintaining a water balance in plants 1

The transpiration stream

Plants require water for many reasons:

- to maintain the **turgor** of their cells
- as a raw material for photosynthesis
- to cool the leaves through the evaporation of water in **transpiration**
- to transport minerals from the roots and dissolved foods throughout the plant.

Water enters plant roots by osmosis from the soil. It is lost by transpiration from the leaves. The **transpiration stream** is the continuous movement of water upwards from the roots to the leaves. Most of this water movement takes place in the vessels of the xylem but the passage of water by osmosis from cell to cell is also involved. Several forces contribute to the transpiration stream:

- **Root pressure** – this is the force created by the continuous entry of water into the root xylem vessels after it has been absorbed from the soil. Root pressure can be enough to push water short distances up the stems of plants.
- **Adhesion** – This is a force of attraction between water molecules and the inner walls of the xylem vessels. It helps to pull the water column up the xylem vessels.
- **Cohesion** – This is a force of attraction between the water molecules themselves. It helps to maintain unbroken water columns as they are pulled upwards to the leaves.
- **Transpiration pull** – The evaporation of water from the leaves causes loss of water from the xylem vessels in the leaf and this creates a suction which pulls the water column in the xylem upwards. This is the main force involved in the upwards movement of water.
- **Osmosis** – concentration gradients exist in the roots and the leaves of plants. In the roots, the high water concentration is in the soil water and the low water concentration is in the cells close to the xylem. Osmosis causes the entry of water from the soil into the root hair cells of the epidermis and then across the cells of the root cortex towards the xylem near the centre.

In the leaves, the high water concentration is in the cells closest to the xylem and the low water concentration is in the spongy mesophyll cells which lose water by evaporation.

movement of water by osmosis across the spongy mesophyll cells of the leaf

evaporation of water from spongy mesophyll cells into leaf air spaces and its diffusion through the stomata out of the leaf

movement of water column up the xylem due to transpiration pull, cohesion, adhesion and root pressure

movement of water by osmosis across the root cortex towards the xylem

entry of water into root hair cell from soil by osmosis

Stomatal mechanism

The stomata on plant leaves are where carbon dioxide enters the plant and where water is lost. The loss of water by transpiration is essential for the uptake and transport of minerals and for the cooling of the leaves. However, the loss must be controlled so that it is not too great to be replaced.

Transpiration rates are higher during the day, when stomata are open to allow the entry of carbon dioxide for photosynthesis. During darkness, photosynthesis stops and there is no requirement for carbon dioxide. Plants are able to reduce unnecessary water loss at night by closing the stomata. The opening and closing of the stomata is caused by the guard cells changing shape.

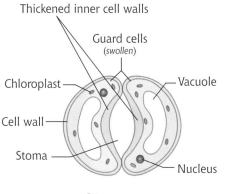

Stoma open

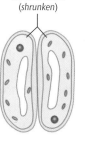

Stoma closed

Top Tip

This is another topic where revision of Standard Grade work can be important. You must be able to relate the structure of a leaf to its functions and also the structure and functions of the xylem and phloem.

During daylight, guard cells gain water by osmosis and swell as they become **turgid**. The thickened inner cell walls cause the cells to bend outwards resulting in the stoma opening. In darkness, the guard cells lose water by osmosis and the cells straighten as they become **flaccid**, resulting in the stoma closing.

Quick Test 21

1. Give two benefits of transpiration to a plant.
2. (a) What is the major force involved in the transpiration stream?
   (b) Name two other forces which contribute to the transpiration stream.
3. The rate of transpiration from a plant can be affected by changes in:

   * temperature
   * wind speed
   * humidity
   * light intensity

   Which of these factors does not cause its effect by altering the rate of evaporation?

Maintaining a water balance in plants 2

Xerophytes

Xerophytes are plants which are adapted to survive in areas where rates of water loss would be too great for other plants. Such areas include deserts, where the hot, dry conditions are a problem, moors, where the exposed windy conditions can cause problems and sand dunes, where the sandy soil does not retain water.

Xerophytes show a range of adaptations which reduce their water loss. These include:

- Stomata that are sunken in pits – this reduces air movement around the stomata and so reduces transpiration.
- Stomata that are protected by hairs – again this reduces air movement around the stomata.
- Rolled leaves – this also protects stomata from air movements, and so reduces transpiration.
- Thick waxy cuticles – these reduce water loss through the leaf epidermis.
- Leaves reduced in size – these have a relatively small surface area and so transpiration is reduced.

Xerophytes may also have root systems adapted to gain as much water as possible. Root adaptations are:

- Superficial roots – these are spread over a large area close to the soil surface, allowing the plant to gain a lot of water whenever there is rain.
- Deep roots – these penetrate deep into the soil to gain water from below ground.

Other xerophytic adaptations include:

- Succulent storage tissue – this allows water to be stored when available and used during dry periods.
- Reversed stomatal opening – stomata may open at night and close during the day to reduce transpiration.
- Low growth habit – plants are sheltered from strong winds and so avoid excessive transpiration.

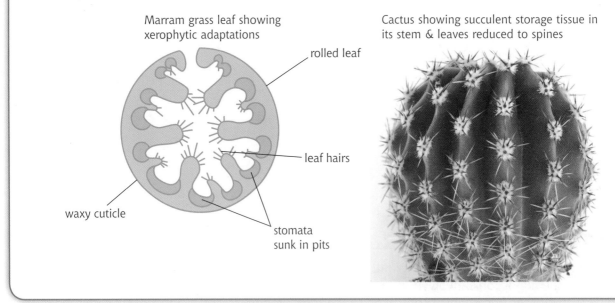

Marram grass leaf showing xerophytic adaptations

rolled leaf

leaf hairs

waxy cuticle

stomata sunk in pits

Cactus showing succulent storage tissue in its stem & leaves reduced to spines

Hydrophytes

Top Tip

Remember, xerophytes are not only plants able to live in areas such as deserts. Many plants living in more moderate conditions may still show xerophytic features.

Hydrophytes are adapted to living partially or totally submerged in water. They have no problems in obtaining water and many do not have a water transport system, since all cells can obtain water directly from the surroundings. The main problem they face is damage caused by the movement of the surrounding water. Their adaptations include:

- Air spaces in the stems and leaves – this increases buoyancy and helps the leaves float upwards towards the light. The air spaces also act as a reservoir of oxygen for respiration and of carbon dioxide for photosynthesis.
- Reduced xylem – found near the centre of the stem rather than near the edges. This increases the flexibility of the stem and reduces the chance of damage by the surrounding water.
- Restricted stomatal distribution – stomata are missing from submerged leaves and found only on the upper surface of floating leaves.

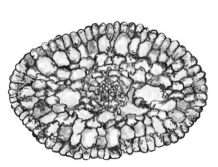

section through a submerged stem, showing air spaces and central vascular tissue

submerged plant stem showing great flexibility

floating leaves of an aquatic plant

Quick Test 22

1. Give an account of transpiration under the following headings:
   (a) the effect of environmental factors on transpiration rate
   (b) the adaptations of xerophytes that reduce transpiration rate
2. (a) Give two reasons why the stem of an aquatic plant contains relatively less xylem than that of a land plant.
   (b) Explain why the vascular tissue of an aquatic plant is found in a single bundle at the centre of the stem, rather than in separate bundles near the edge.

Obtaining food 1

Foraging behaviour and search patterns in animals

Animals are consumers. They must find and eat food in order to gain the energy they need. This involves the animal expending energy. The gain in energy from the food must be more than the energy used in obtaining it. An animal's behaviour is adapted towards this end.

Example – Aquatic flatworms (Planaria)

These animals feed on dead animal remains. They have chemoreceptors on either side of their head. These detect chemicals diffusing from food material. When foraging, flatworms move randomly, but when a food chemical is detected they turn towards the direction of the strongest signal and move towards it. They adjust their direction of movement constantly, producing a zigzag pattern which brings them to the food.

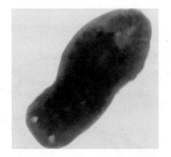

Foraging pattern of flatworm showing random movement until food is detected and then constant adjustment of direction towards food

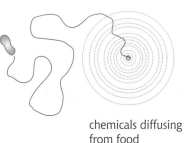

chemicals diffusing from food

Economics of foraging behaviour

Several factors help to determine the best strategy for an animal to take when searching for food. The decisions are instinctive and an animal will alter its strategy automatically to cope with different circumstances. This is called **optimal foraging**. The factors include:

- The relative availability of food – if food is plentiful, then little energy need be spent searching and so the animal can be selective and choose high-quality food. If food is scarce, the animal will eat a mixture of food including some low-quality food, as too much energy would be spent searching for limited quantities of high-quality food.
- The size of the prey – tackling prey which is large may involve the expenditure of too much energy and too great a risk of injury. If the prey is too small, the energy gain will not be worth the energy expenditure.

Competition

If resources are in short supply there will be competition between animals. Two types of competition can occur:

- **Interspecific competition** – this occurs between different species with similar requirements. Inevitably, one species will be a stronger competitor than the other for the common resource. If the resource is very limited, the competition can lead to the weaker competitor declining in number or being forced out of the habitat. In stable ecosystems interspecific competition is kept to a minimum, as different animals occupy different **ecological niches** which reduce overlapping requirements.
- **Intraspecific competition** – this is competition between members of the same species. It is more intense than interspecific competition because the needs of every individual are identical.

Dominance hierarchy

Some species of animals form social groups, for example, breeding herds of red deer and troupes of chimpanzees. In such groups there is usually an accepted order of status, or **dominance hierarchy**. The hierarchy is maintained through ritualised signals of dominance or submission which avoid actual fighting. Benefits of a dominance hierarchy include:

- Reduced risk of injury and energy expenditure.
- Guarantee that the group will have an experienced leader. The leader will have first choice of the resources such as food and mating partners.
- Even the lowest-ranking individual will probably gain more in terms of food and safety than it would on its own.

The hierarchy is not totally static, as younger individuals will challenge for improved positions in the hierarchy and these challenges may lead to real conflict. In some bird species the hierarchy is known as a **pecking order**.

Co-operative hunting

Social groups have allowed some species such as wolves and lions to develop skills as **co-operative hunters**. The techniques differ from species to species, for example wolves wear down their prey with prolonged pursuit, and lions adopt an ambush technique. Whatever method is used, the benefits obtained are common. These include:

- Larger prey can be tackled with a reduced risk of injury.
- A chase can be maintained for longer so that faster prey can be caught.
- All individuals may receive a share of the food even if they were not part of the hunt.

Territorial behaviour

Territorial behaviour is a form of intraspecific competition in which individuals try to establish a defined territory and defend it from other individuals of the species. The purpose is to control an area large enough to provide enough food for the owner of the territory.

Territorial behaviour is easily observed in robins where individual birds defend their own territory in winter and breeding pairs defend a joint territory during the breeding season. The owner or owners will move around the territory displaying and singing as signs of ownership. An intruder will be met with a display of warning signals which will lead to conflict only if the intruder refuses to leave. Benefits of territorial behaviour include:

Top Tip

You must be able to describe the benefits associated with each type of behaviour.

- Reduced risk of injury and energy expenditure.
- The population is distributed in relation to the availability of food.

The size of the territory defended varies with conditions. In years when food is plentiful, the territory need not be so large. When food is scarce, the territory needs to be larger but this requires greater energy expenditure to defend and so decisions about the size of territory defended become more critical.

Obtaining food 2

Sessility in plants

Plants are producers, they manufacture food materials through the process of photosynthesis. This means that they do not need to move about in search of food but instead they are **sessile**, that is they remain in one place.

Competition in plants

Competition, both interspecific and intraspecific, exists between plants growing in the same habitat. Competition is for light, water and soil nutrients. Plants have adaptations which allow them to compete for these resources.

For example, plants can alter their direction of growth or angle their leaves towards the source of light. Plants which grow in shady conditions may contain different proportions of the photosynthetic pigments to enable them to maximise absorption of the light wavelengths which do reach them.

The effect of grazing on plant species diversity

The variety of plant species present in a habitat can be affected by the types of herbivores which graze on them. Sheep are more selective grazers than cattle and so, at low grazing intensity, land grazed by sheep would tend to lose diversity because they would eat more of some species and leave others.

The intensity of grazing can have great effects on the diversity of the grassland. At low intensities of grazing, vigorous-growing plant species are not kept in check and so they will eventually dominate the area, causing less vigorous species to die out and reduce diversity.

High intensities of grazing can cause shortage of food and so all available plant species will be badly affected. Less abundant plant species may be lost altogether, resulting in loss of diversity.

Moderate grazing intensity can increase diversity because the more vigorous plant species are kept in check by the grazers. This allows less vigorous species to become established and thrive.

Compensation point in sun and shade plants

Respiration takes place continually in plants. Over a twenty-four-hour period the rate of respiration is normally higher during the day than at night because of higher temperatures during the day.

Photosynthesis does not take place in darkness. It increases as light intensity increases, reaches a maximum and then decreases as light intensity decreases.

For a plant to grow, the average rate of photosynthesis in twenty-four hours must exceed the average rate of respiration. In other words, the plant must produce more carbohydrate by photosynthesis than it uses in respiration. Twice in a normal twenty-four-hour period the rates of respiration and photosynthesis will be equal. The first time will be in the morning, when photosynthesis is increasing and the second time will be in the evening, when photosynthesis decreases. The light intensity when this happens is called the **compensation point**. The graph below shows compensation points at 8 a.m. and 6 p.m.

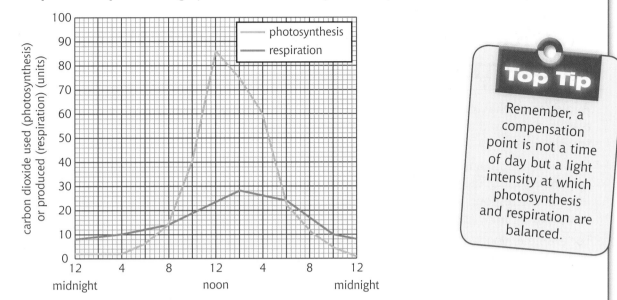

Top Tip

Remember, a compensation point is not a time of day but a light intensity at which photosynthesis and respiration are balanced.

Plants adapted to living in shade conditions have compensation points at lower light intensities than plants adapted to living in full sun conditions. This is essential for the shade plant as it gives it longer in a twenty-four-hour period to carry out enough photosynthesis to supply its needs. Shade plants are able to do this because of the range of photosynthetic pigments they possess.

Quick Test 23

1. African wild dogs are social animals that hunt in packs. They rely on stamina to catch grazing animals such as wildebeest.
   The table shows the effect of wildebeest age on the average duration of successful chases and the percentage hunting success.

Wildebeest age	Stage	Average duration of successful chases (s)	Hunting success (%)
up to 1 year	calves	20	75
from 1–2 years	juveniles	120	50
over 2 years	adults	180	45

   (a) Describe the effect of wildebeest age on the average duration of successful chases.
   (b) Suggest a reason why hunting success is greatest with calves.
   (c) Wild dogs kill a greater number of adult wildebeest than calves.
       Explain this observation in terms of the economics of foraging behaviour.
   (d) State an advantage of co-operative hunting to the wild dogs.
   (e) Following a successful hunt, wild dogs may be displaced from their kill by spotted hyenas. What type of competition does this show?
2. With reference to obtaining food, explain why plants are sessile whereas most animals are mobile.
3. From the graph above at what time of day is the plant showing the greatest net loss of carbohydrate?
4. (a) Which type of plants, sun or shade, are better able to absorb light from the green area of the spectrum?
   (b) Explain why this is necessary.
   (c) Explain why these plants are able to do this.

Coping with dangers 1

Avoidance behaviour and habituation in animals

Avoidance behaviour is any instinctive response which protects an animal from a perceived threat. It is a reflex action and takes place as an automatic response to a stimulus. Such behaviour has an obvious survival value.

However, not all perceived threats are real and an animal could waste a lot of time and energy responding to stimuli which appear threatening but which are harmless. In such cases many animals learn not to respond to a harmless stimulus and to continue with their normal behaviour. This is called **habituation**, and it represents a short-term change in behaviour.

For example, young lambs in a field near a railway track will be startled and run away at their first experience of a train rushing past. However, they soon become accustomed to the regular movement of trains going by the field and they cease to be disturbed by them.

If the stimulus did not occur for some time and then reappeared, the animal would show normal avoidance behaviour and it would take repeated exposure to the stimulus for habituation to be re-established.

Learning as a long-term modification of response

The ability to learn allows some animals to change their behaviour as the result of experience. This has a survival value as the animal learns to avoid dangers and also becomes more efficient at exploiting its environment.

An example of learning to avoid danger happens when a frog catches a wasp to eat, and gets stung. As a result, it learns to avoid trying to eat insects with black and yellow striped bodies. It will also avoid trying to catch other harmless insects with similar markings.

An example of learning to better exploit the environment is shown when seagulls learn to drop mussels from a height in order to break the shells. The birds may be unsuccessful dropping the mussels onto soft ground, but they learn that the shells break if they are dropped onto rocks or concrete.

Individual and social mechanisms for defence

1. Individual mechanisms

The use of teeth and claws are obvious defence methods for some animals, as they make the risk of injury too great for other animals to attack them. Other defence methods include:

- Speed to escape predators, for example gazelles.
- Camouflage to avoid detection, for example stick insects.
- Displays to deter or confuse predators, for example eye-spot markings on the wings of some moths.
- Warning colouration, for example the yellow and black markings of wasps.
- Production of foul-smelling secretions, for example skunks.
- The ability to detach a tail to allow escape, for example some lizards.

2. Social mechanisms

Many animals form groups for defensive reasons. These work in several ways including:

- Large flocks of birds, shoals of fish or herds of wildebeest all reduce the chances of an individual being attacked. There may be earlier detection of a predator by a group than by an individual. Also, the movement of large numbers of potential prey may confuse a predator.
- A group of animals may form a defensive formation. For example, male musk oxen face attacking wolves, forming a defensive barrier of horns to shield calves and females.
- A group of animals may work together to mob and chase potential predators. For example, crows and gulls may harass a wide range of other animals including birds of prey, snakes and foxes.

Top Tip

Remember that social behaviour also has some drawbacks, for instance there is increased intraspecific competition for food and disease is more likely to spread quickly.

Quick Test 24

1. Which of the following best describes habituation?
   A The same escape response is performed repeatedly.
   B The same response is always given to the same stimulus.
   C A harmless stimulus ceases to produce a response.
   D Behaviour is reinforced by regular repetition.

2. Hawks are predators which attack flocks of pigeons. The graph (right) shows how attack success by a hawk varies with the number of pigeons in a flock.
   Which of the following statements could explain the observations shown in the graph?
   A A hawk only needs to eat a small percentage of a large flock of prey.
   B Co-operative hunting is more effective with small numbers of prey.
   C A predator can be more selective when prey numbers increase.
   D A hawk has difficulty focusing on one pigeon in a large flock.

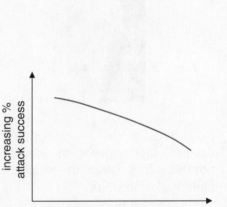

3. Fulmars and common terns are seabirds that breed in large social groups.
   (a) The table compares breeding in these birds.

Feature of breeding	Fulmar	Common Tern
nest distribution and location	crowded on cliff ledges	scattered on pebble beaches
egg number and colour	single white egg	three speckled eggs
chick behaviour	remains in nest until able to fly	can move short distance from nest soon after hatching

   (i) Using information from the table, explain why fulmars are less vulnerable to predation than common terns.
   (ii) Suggest how features of common tern eggs and chicks may increase their survival chances.
   (b) Explain how living in large social groups may help animals in defence against predators.

Coping with dangers 2

Structural defence mechanisms in plants

Cellular defence mechanisms for plants have already been covered in Unit 1.

Examples of structural defence mechanisms include:

- The tough bark of trees protects underlying living tissues.
- The stings of nettles contain a mixture of irritating chemicals which deter many grazing animals.
- The spines of gorse bushes and cacti protect the plants from being eaten.
- The thorns of roses and brambles offer similar protection.

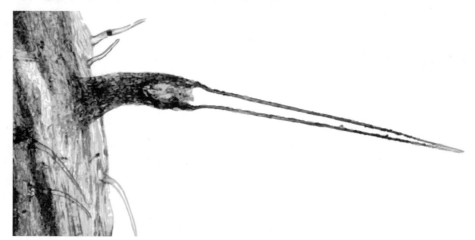

Sting of a nettle plant

Holly trees are well known for their spiny leaves. It is said that the number of spines on the leaves decreases the higher up the leaves grow. Many investigations have been carried out to check whether or not this is true. Often, the results do not confirm the suggestion and many low-growing leaves are found with few or no spines.

There are probably several factors which affect the results of such investigations. These are:

- Ornamental varieties of holly, bred for gardens and parks probably do not show the same growth patterns as native wild varieties
- The number of spines is related to the age and size of the leaf with older, bigger leaves losing spines as they grow
- Trees that suffer grazing damage will tend to have younger, spinier leaves near the ground
- Holly leaves are dropped from the tree after two or three years and so there will be a mixture of leaves of different ages at all heights.

The ability to tolerate grazing

Top Tip

Many plants are eaten by herbivores but they are adapted to cope with this. Examples of how this is achieved include:

- Grasses have their growth points (meristems) very low near the soil surface at the base of the stems. This means that they are missed by grazing animals and leaves can continue to grow from the bottom, even though the tips have been eaten.
- Some grasses and other plants have underground stems. These can spread and produce new aerial shoots and leaves even if previous aerial parts have been totally destroyed.
- Some plants, such as daisies and plantain, avoid being completely eaten by forming a flattened rosette of leaves close to the soil surface.
- Many plants have great powers of regeneration. Even small pieces of root tissue left in the soil are enough to allow the development of complete plants.

Be careful when answering questions on structural and cellular defence mechanisms in plants as some can easily be confused. For example, stings are described as structural mechanisms even though they contain defensive chemicals produced by cells. This is because the defensive mechanism involves a purpose-built structure.

Galls are described as cellular mechanisms even though the gall is a structure. This is because the mechanism is a response by cells to an invading organism.

Plantain showing a rosette of leaves

Quick Test 25

1. Describe two adaptations of grass plants which help them to survive grazing by herbivores.
2. The leaves of plantains form rosettes which are flattened close to the ground and which are arranged with minimal overlap.
   Explain two ways in which this leaf arrangement is of benefit to the plant.
3. Describe two ways in which the spines of the cactus plant in the photograph below help to conserve the water stored in its stem.

Growth differences between plants and animals 1

Meristems

The growth of an organism depends on cell division by mitosis. New cells are produced and these grow to full size. One of the main differences in the growth of animals and plants is that plants have localised areas of growth whereas animal growth takes place throughout the body.

Plants possess **meristems**. These are regions of actively dividing cells. The new cells produced elongate and cause an increase in length. The growing cells also become differentiated to perform specialised functions. Meristems are found in a number of places in plants:

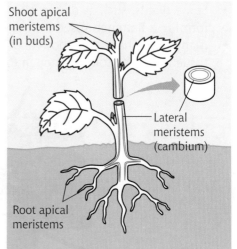

Shoot apical meristems (in buds)

Lateral meristems (cambium)

Root apical meristems

- **Apical meristems** – these are found at the growing tips of roots and shoots and in buds. They are responsible for increases in the length of shoots and roots and for the growth of side branches and leaves.

- **Lateral meristems** – the main lateral meristem is the **cambium**, which is found in between the phloem and xylem tissues of the stem and root. This is responsible for increases in the width of a plant. It leads to the formation of the wood of plants such as trees which live for many years.

Formation of annual rings

Growth resulting from the activity of the apical meristems is known as **primary growth**. The xylem and phloem tissues which form as part of this growth are known as **primary xylem** and **primary phloem**.

Growth resulting from the activity of the cambium is called **secondary growth**. The xylem and phloem tissues which form as part of this growth are called **secondary xylem** and **secondary phloem**.

Secondary growth begins when the cambium divides in such a way that it extends beyond the xylem and phloem to produce a complete circle of cambium in the stem of the plant. Continued division of the cambium then produces new cells, some of which differentiate into secondary phloem to the outside of the cambium circle and some of which differentiate into secondary xylem to the inside.

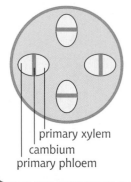

primary xylem
cambium
primary phloem

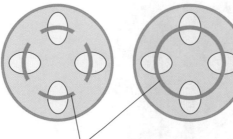

cambium extending beyond the xylem and phloem to form a complete circle

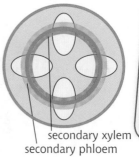

secondary xylem
secondary phloem

Top Tip

Be sure to revise the Standard Grade work on the structure and function of the xylem and phloem.

Much more secondary xylem is produced than secondary phloem. As the xylem vessels age they become filled with **lignin** and become the wood which supports the tree. Only the youngest xylem functions as transporting tissue.

In temperate countries like Britain, the activity of the cambium varies during the year. In spring the cambium is very active and the xylem vessels formed at this time are large with a wide diameter. As the year passes, the activity of the cambium slows. The summer xylem vessels have a smaller diameter and are more densely packed. Activity stops during winter until the following spring, when renewed cambium activity produces wide xylem vessels once again.

narrower diameter summer xylem vessels

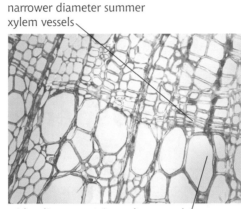

wider diameter spring xylem vessels produced the following year

cambium

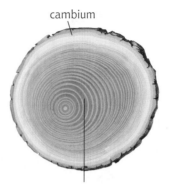

annual ring - each ring contains one year's growth of xylem including the light coloured spring xylem and the darker summer xylem

The difference between the xylem vessels produced late one year and the adjacent xylem vessels produced early the next year is clearly visible and allows the annual growth rings in the cross section of a tree to be counted.

Quick Test 26

1. The root of a germinating bean seed was marked with ink at 1 mm intervals along its length. The seed was allowed to grow for a further three days. The positions of the marks at the start and after the three days are shown in the diagrams.

    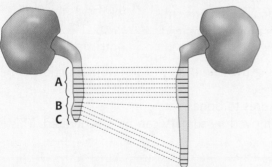

    (a) Explain the change in relative positions of the marks in region B of the root.
    (b) Which letter identifies the region of the root containing the meristem?
    (c) Explain why there has been no increase in length in region A of the root.

    Diagram A **Diagram B**

2. Diagram A shows a section through a woody stem.
    Diagram B shows a magnified view of the area indicated on the section.
    (a) Which letter on diagram B shows the position of a lateral meristem?
    (b) Name the tissue of which annual rings are composed.
    (c) In which season was the woody stem cut? Explain your choice.

J   K   L M N

Growth differences between plants and mammals 2

Regeneration in angiosperms and mammals

Regeneration is the ability to replace lost or damaged parts. Angiosperms (flowering plants) often show extensive powers of regeneration. Parts of plants, such as fragments of roots left in the soil or pieces of shoots that have been broken off, can often grow replacement shoots or roots. These develop from meristematic tissue which forms a bank of undifferentiated cells in the fragment. Eventually a complete new plant will form.

The ability of plants to regenerate is important, because it allows them to recover from damage caused by herbivores. It also has a commercial importance because it allows people to produce many new plants from an existing one by artificial methods. The offspring produced by cuttings and by other artificial forms of vegetative propagation are genetically identical to the parents. Therefore they will show the same characteristics.

Cutting of a Basil plant with new roots

Modern propagation techniques using **tissue cultures** also depend on the regenerative ability of plants.

Tissue culture involves taking some meristematic cells from a plant and placing them on sterile agar gel. They are then treated with a plant growth substance to stimulate them to divide into a mass of undifferentiated cells called a **callus**. Further treatment stimulates the growth of shoots and roots to produce a small plant, genetically identical to the original plant. This technique allows the production of large numbers of identical plants.

Regeneration in mammals is much more limited. This is because mammals do not possess significant areas of undifferentiated cells equivalent to a meristem. However, there are some important examples of the regeneration of damaged tissue which can occur in mammals:

- **Skin** – a layer of cells in the skin is capable of increasing the rate of new skin-cell production to heal wounds to the skin.
- **Bones** – new bone cells can be produced to heal fractures to bones.
- **Liver** – areas of liver which have been damaged or removed by surgery can be regenerated. This is because liver cells are relatively unspecialised.

Growth patterns in plants and animals

The growth of an organism can be measured in a number of ways.

- **Mass** – for many organisms the simplest method is to record the change in mass over time. This has the disadvantage that mass can vary significantly because of short-term variations in the water content of the organism.
- **Height** – recording the change in height over time is suitable for some organisms but not all, because it ignores changes in width.
- **Dry mass** – recording the change in dry mass over time is the most accurate measure of growth but it involves killing the organism by drying it and so it can only be done once. It is normally used

for small plants where samples of the plants are taken at different stages of growth and average dry masses are measured for each stage.

Most organisms show an initial period of slow growth followed by a period of faster growth and a final period where growth slows and stops as the maximum size is reached. There are variations to this general pattern that are typical for different groups of organisms. The actual method used to measure the growth depends on the type of organism involved.

Human growth curve

Body mass (kg) vs Time (years)

- adolescent growth spurt
- infant growth spurt

0 5 10 15 20 25
Time (years)

Insect growth curve (e.g. locust)

Length (units) vs Time (days)

Growth is restricted to short periods after the old exoskeleton is shed and before the soft underlying new exoskeleton hardens.

Annual plant growth curve

Dry mass (units) vs Time (months)

Perennial plant growth curve (e.g. tree)

Height (units) vs Time (years)

The initial decease is due to the food store of the seed being used up before the plant is able to photosynthesise.

The final decrease is due to the dispersal of seeds from the plant and its death after one season's growth.

The overall pattern of growth shows a continual increase in size until a maximum is reached. The plant then remains at this size until it dies.

The step-like pattern is due to periods of dormancy each winter.

> **Top Tip**
>
> Remember, the basis for regeneration and all forms of vegetative propagation is cell division by mitosis. This accounts for the fact that offspring will be genetically identical to the parent.

Quick Test 27

1. (a) Explain why increase in dry mass is a better measure of plant growth than increase in fresh mass.
   (b) Explain why increase in dry mass cannot be used to measure the growth of an individual plant.
   (c) Explain how this problem is overcome when dry mass is used as a measure of growth.

2.

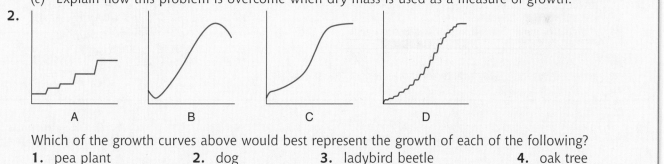

A   B   C   D

Which of the growth curves above would best represent the growth of each of the following?
1. pea plant   2. dog   3. ladybird beetle   4. oak tree

Genetic control 1

The Jacob-Monod model of gene action in bacteria

Growth and development is influenced by a number of factors including the genetic information present in the cells. Every body-cell of an organism contains the same genetic information but not all the information will be needed by all cells. Therefore there must be mechanisms which allow the correct genes to function at the correct time. One such mechanism has been demonstrated in the bacterium *Escherichia coli (E. coli)*. This is known as the **Jacob-Monod model of gene action**.

E. coli is able to produce an enzyme which breaks down lactose sugar into the simpler sugars glucose and galactose. The enzyme is only produced if lactose is present and so there must be a mechanism to prevent the production of the enzyme when it is not needed. The mechanism involves three structures situated on the bacterial chromosome:

- A **regulator gene** – this codes for the production of a **repressor** protein molecule.
- The **operator** – this acts as an on/off switch for the structural gene.
- A **structural** gene – this codes for the production of the enzyme.

Together these associated structures are known as an **operon**.

The mechanism works in the following way:

- If lactose is absent –

  1. The regulator gene codes for the production of a repressor protein molecule.

  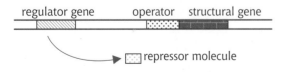

  2. The repressor molecule binds with the operator. This prevents the structural gene from being switched on and no enzyme is produced

- If lactose is present –

  1. The regulator gene codes for the production of a repressor protein molecule.

Top Tip

If asked about the details of the mechanism, remember that the production of the repressor protein and of the enzyme require all the steps involved in protein synthesis. These are:

- the production of appropriate mRNA molecules from the regulator gene and the structural gene respectively
- the passage of the mRNA from the nucleus to the ribosomes in the cytoplasm of the cell
- the assembly of the repressor molecule and the enzyme at the ribosomes using amino acids carried by appropriate tRNA molecules.

You will not be asked for the names of the sugars which are the products of the breakdown of lactose.

2. The repressor molecule binds with some lactose rather than with the operator. The operator can now switch on the structural gene, which then codes for the production of the enzyme.

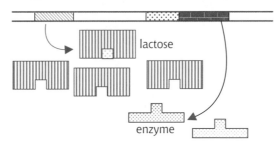

3. The enzyme binds with the lactose and breaks it down into glucose and galactose.

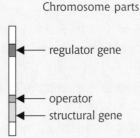

glucose   galactose

The lactose acts as the **inducer** because it induces the production of enzyme.

When all the lactose has been broken down, the repressor molecules will again bind with the operator. The structural gene will be switched off and the production of the enzyme will stop.

This mechanism is a benefit to the bacteria because it means that the enzyme is only produced when it is needed. This saves energy and avoids the needless use of resources such as amino acids.

Quick Test 28

1. The diagram shows parts of the chromosome of the bacterium *E. coli*. The list has three molecules involved in the control of lactose metabolism.

Chromosome parts   List of molecules

regulator gene

                                    lactose-digesting enzyme
                                    repressor
operator   inducer
structural gene

(a) Say whether each of the following statements is **True** or **False** if lactose is present or absent in the medium in which *E. coli* is growing.

	Statement	Lactose present	Lactose absent
(i)	Regulator gene codes for the repressor molecule	True or False	True or False
(ii)	Repressor molecule binds to the inducer	True or False	True or False
(iii)	Repressor molecule binds to the operator	True or False	True or False
(iv)	Structural gene is switched on	True or False	True or False
(v)	Structural gene codes for the enzyme	True or False	True or False

(b) Name the inducer molecule.
(c) Give one advantage to *E. coli* of having this type of genetic control system.

Genetic control 2

The part played by genes in controlling metabolic pathways

Most processes taking place in living cells involve a metabolic pathway of several stages. Each stage of the pathway is a chemical reaction requiring a specific enzyme to control it. If one enzyme is not produced or does not function properly because of a genetic fault, then the sequence of reactions will be disrupted. This is called a **metabolic block**.

For example, **phenylketonuria** (PKU) is a rare inherited metabolic disorder that can result in several neurological problems. People with this condition have problems breaking down and using the amino acid phenylalanine.

Phenylalanine is obtained from protein in our diet but there is normally an excess which is broken down to another amino acid called tyrosine.

Tyrosine has several functions. It is used in the production of a number of chemicals needed for the correct transfer of nerve signals. It is also needed for the formation of the skin pigment melanin and for the hormone thyroxine.

The metabolic pathway involved is shown below.

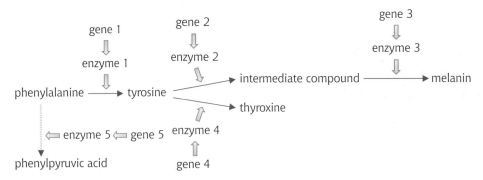

In PKU, enzyme 1 is not produced due to a mutation in gene 1. As a result, phenylalanine accumulates in the blood. Some phenylalanine is converted to phenylpyruvic acid by enzyme 5. Excess phenylalanine and phenylpyruvic acid disrupts normal brain development.

People with PKU tend to be paler than normal because levels of melanin are reduced due to the lack of tyrosine. Some melanin can be produced by other chemical pathways.

PKU can be detected shortly after birth by a routine test. If it is detected, the baby will be kept on a low phenylalanine diet so that brain development can take place normally.

Note that if a mutation of gene 3 prevents the production of enzyme 3, the result will be albinism, because no melanin will be produced.

The control of cell differentiation

During the development of an organism, cells become differentiated to perform different specialised functions. All the cells of an organism contain the same genetic information. Therefore some of the genes must operate in some cells to control their development into a particular cell type whereas, in other cells, other genes must operate to control their development into different cell types. This is called **gene expression** and it means that there must be a mechanism to make some genes active but not others.

If genes are switched on or off at particular key stages of cell development then the way in which the cell develops can be controlled. Other genes switching on at successive stages will fine-tune the development of cells into various specialised cells and tissues.

Stem cells are undifferentiated cells in the body. They can divide to produce new cells which are capable of differentiation. It is hoped research on stem cells and on the mechanisms involved in switching genes on or off will lead to treatments for a range of conditions, including cancer, Parkinson's disease and spinal cord injuries.

Top Tip

Remember, there will be some genes that are always switched on in all the cells of an organism. These will be the genes which code for enzymes needed for essential processes such as respiration.

There will be genes that are switched on only in particular cells and never in others. For example, the gene controlling insulin production will only be switched on in some pancreas cells.

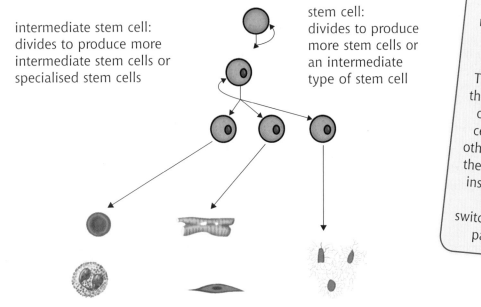

intermediate stem cell: divides to produce more intermediate stem cells or specialised stem cells

stem cell: divides to produce more stem cells or an intermediate type of stem cell

specialised stem cells: divide to produce specialised cells, for example:

blood stem cells ⟶ different types of blood cells

muscle stem cells ⟶ different types of muscle cells

bone stem cells ⟶ different types of bone cells

Quick Test 29

1. Bone cells differ from liver cells because:
   A their chromosome complements are different
   B they contain genes for different characteristics
   C different genes have been switched on as they developed
   D they have different proportions of dominant and recessive alleles of the genes
2. Phenylketonurea is a disorder caused by:
   A lack of melanin in the skin
   B a gene mutation
   C lack of phenylalanine in the diet
   D a chromosomal mutation
3. Part of a metabolic pathway involving the amino acids phenylalanine is shown in the diagram.

   digestion of protein ⟶ phenylalanine —(enzyme A)⟶ tyrosine —(enzyme B)⟶ other compounds in the diet

   Phenylketonurea (PKU) is an inherited condition in which enzyme A is either absent or does not function. Predict the effect on the concentration of phenylalanine and tyrosine if enzyme A is absent.

Hormonal influences 1

Pituitary hormones

The **pituitary gland** is attached to the **hypothalamus** of the brain. One example of a pituitary hormone, ADH (antidiuretic hormone), has already been covered at Standard Grade. The pituitary gland produces several more hormones which are important in the development and proper functioning of the body. Two further examples are:

1. **Human growth hormone** (GH). This hormone has a direct effect on the growth of the body by stimulating the growth of bone, cartilage and muscle in children. It does this by increasing the uptake of amino acids by the cells and increasing protein synthesis. As an individual matures, the production of GH is reduced.

   A deficiency of GH during childhood can result in growth problems.

   If GH deficiency is identified in children, it can be successfully treated using human growth hormone. The only supply of this used to be from the pituitary gland of a corpse, but now it can be produced by genetically modified bacteria.

2. **Thyroid stimulating hormone** (TSH). This hormone stimulates the **thyroid gland** in the neck to produce the hormone **thyroxine**. Thyroxine has an important role in controlling the metabolic rate.

   TSH production by the pituitary gland and thyroxine production by the thyroid gland are regulated by a negative feedback system. High levels of thyroxine in the blood cause the pituitary gland to reduce production of TSH. This causes the thyroid gland to produce less thyroxine and so the pituitary gland increases TSH production.

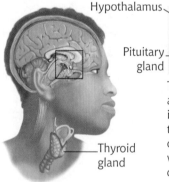

Hypothalamus

Pituitary gland

Thyroid gland

The hypothalamus and the pituitary in the brain control the normal secretion of thyroid hormones, which in turn control metabolism

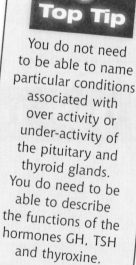

Top Tip

You do not need to be able to name particular conditions associated with over activity or under-activity of the pituitary and thyroid glands. You do need to be able to describe the functions of the hormones GH, TSH and thyroxine.

Quick Test 30

1. The production of thyroxine in mammals is controlled by the hormone TSH. Thyroxine controls metabolic rate in body cells and has a negative feedback effect on gland X.
The diagram below shows the relationship between TSH and thyroxine production.

   (a) Name gland X

   (b) In an investigation into the effects of thyroxine, groups of rats of similar mass were treated as follows.

   Group A were fed a normal diet.
   Group B were fed a normal diet plus thyroxine.
   Group C were fed a normal diet plus an inhibitor of thyroxine production.

   The table below shows the average hourly oxygen consumption in cm³ per gram of body mass in rats from each group.

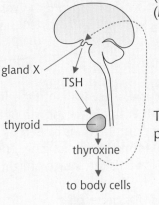

Group	Average hourly oxygen consumption (cm³g⁻¹)
A	1·6
B	2·8
C	1·2

   (i) Explain how the results in the table support the statement that an increase in metabolic rate leads to an increase in oxygen consumption.

   (ii) What evidence suggests that rats fed on a normal diet make thyroxine?

   (iii) How would the level of TSH production in group A compare with group C?

   (iv) Calculate the percentage decrease in oxygen consumption which results from feeding thyroxine inhibitor to rats.

   (v) The table below relates to aspects of the appearance and behaviour of rats in groups B and C.

Group	Appearance of ears and feet	Behaviour
B	pink	lie stretched out
C	pale	lie curled up with feet tucked in

   Complete the following sentences by choosing one of the alternatives in each pair.

   1. Compared with rats in group B, the rats in group C have a (higher/lower) metabolic rate and show (dilation/constriction) of skin blood vessels.

   2. The behaviour of rats in group C allows them to (lose/conserve) body heat.

2. Give an account of the role of the pituitary gland in controlling normal growth and development.

Hormonal influences 2

Plant growth substances

The growth and development of plants is also affected by the production of hormones, although these are often referred to as plant growth substances. Two examples are:

1. **Indole acetic acid** (IAA). This is one of a group of similar chemicals called **auxins**. IAA is produced in the meristems of plants, particularly in the tips of roots and shoots, the buds, the growing points of leaves and in seeds.

It can diffuse from where it is produced to neighbouring cells and it can also be transported in the phloem. IAA has many functions including:

- Stimulating the cells in the apical meristems to divide by mitosis.
- Stimulating newly formed cells to elongate.
- Promoting the differentiation of newly formed cells into specialised cell types.
- Promoting apical dominance by inhibiting the growth of lateral (side) buds in favour of the apical bud. If the apical bud is damaged the inhibition is removed and lateral buds will take over the growth.
- Preventing leaf fall during the growing season by inhibiting the formation of an abscission layer in the leaf stalks. IAA levels decrease in autumn and the inhibition is removed. The abscission layer forms in the leaf stalks and this allows the stalk to snap, causing leaf fall.
- Stimulating fruit formation. IAA from the seeds stimulates development of the ovary wall into the fruit.
- Producing **tropic movements**. Tropisms are growth movements of plants, for example the growth of a shoot in a curve so that it grows towards the source of light (positive phototropism). This is caused by an unequal distribution of IAA in the region behind the meristem where newly formed cells elongate. This produces unequal growth and causes the growing shoot to grow in a curve towards the source of light.

Top Tip

Remember that the general definition of a hormone is a chemical which is produced at one site and which has an effect at another site. Apply this definition to all the examples covered – both plant and animal.

direction of light from one side

shoot tip

IAA diffuses down to area of cell elongation but concentrates more on shaded side

shaded side has greater cell elongation and so shoot grows in a curve towards the light

The cause of the uneven distribution of IAA which results in the tropic responses has been the subject of much research. The mechanisms involved differ in the various forms of tropisms.

In low concentrations, IAA promotes growth but in high concentrations it inhibits growth. This fact is utilised with synthetic versions of auxins, which are used in a number of ways, including:

- As rooting powders which promote root growth on cuttings.
- As selective weedkillers on lawns. Broad-leaved weeds absorb more of the chemical than narrow-leaved grasses and so their growth is inhibited.
- To induce fruit formation without the need for pollination. This produces seedless fruits.

2. **Gibberellic acid** (GA) is one of a group of chemicals known as gibberellins.

It has a number of specific roles, including:

- Ensuring normal growth height by causing the cells in the internodes of plants to elongate and increase in length. Dwarf varieties of plants (such as dwarf pea plants) are caused by the lack of gibberellic acid. Dwarf varieties can be made to grow to normal height by the application of gibberellic acid.
- Breaking the dormancy of buds after a period of inactivity over winter.
- Promoting the germination of cereal grains. Gibberellic acid is produced in the embryo of the grain when the grain absorbs water after a period of dormancy. It diffuses to a layer of cells called the

aleurone layer, which surrounds the starchy food store. Here it switches on the gene which codes for amylase production. The amylase will then digest the starch into maltose for the embryo to use in respiration to provide the energy needed for germination. Brewers sometime use gibberellic acid to induce germination of barley grains for malting.

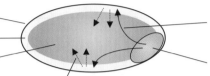

seed coat

aleurone layer

starch food store

production of gibberellic acid by embryo and its diffusion to the aleurone layer

embryo

production of amylase by the aleurone layer resulting in the digestion of starch to maltose

Quick Test 31

1. An investigation was carried out into the effect of different concentrations of IAA on growth in length of shoot tips.
   Two 10 mm lengths of shoot tip tissue were immersed in solutions containing different concentrations of IAA.
   A control experiment was set up with two 10 mm lengths of shoot tip tissue immersed in distilled water.
   The results obtained are shown in the table below.
   Promotion (+) in growth is obtained when the growth is greater than in the control.
   Inhibition (−) in growth is obtained when the growth is less than in the control.

increasing concentration

Concentration of IAA solution (molar)	Average length of shoot after 24 hours (mm)	Average difference in length compared to control (mm)
Control	12·0	
10^{-9}	12·0	0·0
10^{-8}	13·0	+1·0
10^{-7}	14·0	+2·0
10^{-6}	15·0	+3·0
10^{-5}	16·0	+4·0
10^{-4}	14·5	+2·5
10^{-3}	13·0	+1·0
10^{-2}	12·0	0·0
10^{-1}	11·0	−1·0

(a) Identify the range of IAA concentrations that promote shoot growth.
(b) State one way in which the design of the experiment could be changed to improve the reliability of the results.
(c) Predict the effect of an IAA concentration of 10^{-10} on shoot growth.
(d) Explain why −2 mm would be the greatest value for inhibition of growth in the shoots.
(e) Suggest why the shoot tips were left in the solutions for twenty-four hours.
(f) Why must the tissue used in the investigation be taken from the tip of the shoot?
2. Give three uses of synthetic plant hormones.

Environmental influences 1

The importance of individual macro-elements in plants

Some mineral elements are needed in relatively large quantities by plants. These are referred to as **macro-**elements. The need for specific mineral elements can be demonstrated using **water culture** experiments. In these, plants are grown in carefully controlled conditions in which all their mineral nutrients are supplied from a range of prepared solutions. Each solution lacks one of the essential elements. A control solution contains all the elements. Therefore any abnormal growth characteristics shown by the plants must be due to a deficiency of the missing element.

Top Tip

Make sure you can explain the reasons for the aeration tube and the light-proof cover in water culture investigations. Make sure you can give a reason for an observed deficiency symptom.

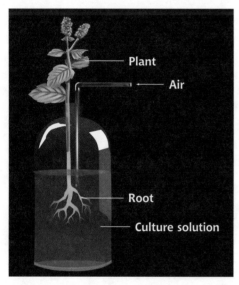

Plant

Air

Root

Culture solution

The air tube allows the culture solution to be aerated so that the roots receive oxygen – needed for active uptake of minerals.

The container would be covered with a light-proof material to prevent algal growth in the culture solution.

The following photographs of leaves from tomato plants show symptoms caused by a deficiency of one important mineral element.

Control

nitrogen

Deficiency of:

phosphorus

potassium

magnesium

The deficiency symptoms and the reasons for them, for each of these elements are shown in the table.

Mineral element	Deficiency symptoms	Reasons
Nitrogen	Extremely stunted growth. Chlorosis – yellowing of the leaves. Red leaf bases.	Nitrogen is part of proteins, nucleic acids, chlorophyll and many other compounds.
Phosphorus	Stunted growth. Dull green leaves. Red leaf bases.	Phosphorus is part of nucleic acids, ATP and many other intermediates of respiration and photosynthesis.
Potassium	Extremely stunted growth. Leaves go yellow at edges and die early.	Potassium is needed for the activation of many enzymes, stomata opening and closing and the transport of chemicals across membranes.
Magnesium	Chlorosis. Poor growth.	Magnesium is part of the chlorophyll molecule.

Quick Test 32

1. The diagram below shows the apparatus used to investigate the growth of oat seedlings in water culture solutions. Each solution lacks one element required for normal growth.
   The containers were painted black to prevent algal growth.

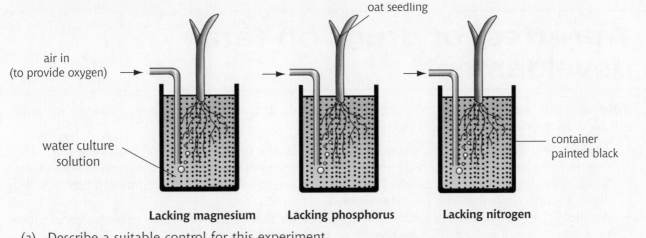

(a) Describe a suitable control for this experiment.
(b) Suggest a reason why algal growth should be prevented in the culture solutions.
(c) (i) Which of the solutions would produce plants with red leaf bases?
   (ii) Which of the solutions would produce plants with chlorotic leaves?
(d) Name a magnesium-containing molecule found in oat seedlings.
(e) Explain why the uptake of elements by oat seedling roots is dependent on the availability of oxygen.

Environmental influences 2

The importance of individual macro-elements in animals

Examples of mineral elements important to animals include iron and calcium.

- **Iron** is a part of the haemoglobin molecule and so it is essential for the transport of oxygen by the red blood cells. Deficiency of iron can cause anaemia. It is also part of the hydrogen carrier proteins of the cytochrome system and so it is needed for normal respiration.
- **Calcium**, in the form of calcium phosphate, is a component of bones, teeth and shells. It is also needed for the transmission of nerve impulses, for blood clotting and for muscle contraction.

Some minerals can be harmful. For example, the metal lead is toxic. It is known to inhibit enzyme activity in both plants and animals.

Lead is no longer used for water pipes, as a component of paints or as an additive to petrol.

The effect of vitamin D deficiency in humans

We obtain the calcium we need from our food. Dairy products and green vegetables are good sources of calcium. The efficient absorption of calcium from the small intestine and the utilisation of the calcium by the bone-forming cells both require vitamin D. If this vitamin is absent during childhood growth, it can lead to **rickets**, a condition in which bone fails to harden. Rickets is particularly evident if the leg bones bend outwards. This is because the leg bones are not strong enough to support the weight of the body.

The effect of drugs on fetal development

Many substances can pass across the placenta from the blood system of a pregnant woman to the fetus and harm its development. Examples of such substances include:

- **Thalidomide** – This drug was introduced in the 1950s as a treatment for morning sickness in pregnant women. An unknown side-effect of the drug was that it disrupted the development of the limbs of the fetus. Many children were born with severe deformities of their arms and legs. The drug was withdrawn from use with pregnant women.
- **Alcohol** – Pregnant women are advised not to drink alcohol at all. The effects of high alcohol intake on a fetus are well known, whereas the effects of low intake are unclear. The advice is that it is better to be safe and avoid any risk of adverse effects.

  It is known that drinking alcohol during the first three months of pregnancy can damage the developing organs and nervous system of a fetus. Continued drinking can lead to **fetal alcohol syndrome** which causes several symptoms in the baby including: low birth weight; facial abnormalities; retarded growth and mental development.

- **Nicotine** – There are many harmful chemicals in cigarette smoke including tar, carbon monoxide and nicotine. Nicotine is very poisonous and affects the development of the fetus. It causes premature births, underweight babies, retarded growth and mental development.

  Nicotine is also extremely addictive and it easily passes across the placenta. This results in babies being born with nicotine addiction. They must then face the traumas of withdrawal along with any other problems they may have. The use of nicotine replacement therapies as an aid to stopping smoking can also cause these problems.

Top Tip

The effect of lead as an enzyme inhibitor can easily be demonstrated by using a dilute solution of a lead salt to slow down the appearance of brown colouration on the cut surface of a fruit such as an apple. The brown colour is the result of the enzyme catechol oxidase, which oxidises catechol into a brown-coloured compound which helps protect the damaged tissue from bacterial attack.

Quick Test 33

1. Many substances affect growth and development in humans.
   Name the chemical from Table 1 to match its role in, or effect on, growth and development described in Table 2.
   Each chemical may be used **once, more than once** or **not at all**.
   The numbers in brackets indicate how many chemicals are involved.

Table 1

| Calcium |
| Nicotine |
| Alcohol |
| Vitamin D |
| Lead |
| Thalidomide |
| Magnesium |
| Iron |

Table 2

Inhibits activity of certain enzymes.	(1)
Required for the uptake of calcium from the small intestine.	(1)
Required for normal growth of teeth and bones.	(2)
Required for haemoglobin synthesis.	(1)
Retards both physical growth and mental development of the human embryo.	(2)

2. The table below shows the relationship between the concentration of lead in the placenta and the average birth mass of human babies.

Range of concentration of lead in placenta (units)	Average birth mass (kg)
25–29	2·32
20–24	2·87
15–19	3·40
10–14	3·74
5–9	4·40

   (a) (i) Describe the relationship between the concentration of placental lead and average birth mass.
   (ii) State the effect of lead on cell functions.
   (b) (i) Describe the effect of thalidomide on fetal development.
   (ii) Name two drugs which have the effect of causing a decrease in the expected birth mass.

Environmental influences 3

The influence of light on plants

1. Etiolation and tropisms

Light is a major influence on the growth of vegetative shoots (leafy shoots which do not produce flowers).

When plants are grown in darkness, their shoots are longer and thinner than if they were grown in light. Their leaves remain small and yellow rather than fully developed and green. This state is called **etiolation** and it is an adaptation which increases the chance of a plant, particularly a seedling, growing in darkness to reach light. If it does so, growth will become normal.

The direction of growth is also influenced by light. If a growing plant is receiving light from one side, the growth will take place in a curve so that the shoot grows towards the light. Growth movements such as this are called **tropic responses**. This example is called **positive phototropism** because the growth is towards the stimulus (light).

Tropic responses involve the plant growth substance IAA. (See page 72)

2. Flowering

The number of hours of daylight in a twenty-four-hour period, or photoperiod, is the most consistent factor associated with seasonal change. The flowering of many plants is controlled by changes in the photoperiod. This is known as **photoperiodism**. Some species are classed as **short-day plants** and their flowering is in response to decreasing photoperiods. Other species are **long-day plants**. These flower as a response to increasing photoperiods. Many species are **day neutral** because their flowering is not controlled by the photoperiod at all.

Each long-day or short-day species has a **critical period**. Long-day plants begin flowering when the photoperiod exceeds their critical period and short-day plants begin flowering when the photoperiod falls below their critical period.

It is now known that the mechanism involved has more to do with the length of darkness than the length of daylight in a twenty-four-hour period. Therefore a long-day plant would be better described as a short-night plant and a short-day plant as a long-night plant. However, the old terminology is still used.

The natural distribution of long-day plants tends to be in temperate latitudes (i.e. outside the tropics) because these regions have greater variation in the photoperiod and so increasing photoperiods are more distinct. Their flowering is initiated in spring as photoperiods increase.

Short-day plants tend to be found naturally in equatorial and tropical regions, where photoperiods vary less. Here they are able to flower throughout the year. Some are found in temperate regions where they begin flowering in autumn as photoperiods decrease.

The effect of light on breeding in birds and mammals

Animals also respond to changes in the photoperiod. This acts as a **trigger stimulus** for rhythmical behaviour patterns which show an annual cycle.

In birds and many small mammals, their reproductive systems become active as the result of increasing photoperiods in spring. This means that the offspring are born at a time when conditions are warmer and food is plentiful.

Top Tip

Photoperiod changes are also involved in other examples of annual behaviour patterns of animals, such as hibernation and migration. Be prepared to explain the benefit to the animal of any such behaviour.

In larger mammals, the decreasing photoperiods of autumn provide the stimulus for breeding. The longer gestation period of these animals means that the young are born in the following spring when conditions are warmer and food is plentiful.

These patterns of breeding behaviour increase the chances of survival of the offspring.

Quick Test 34

1. Etiolation is a survival adaptation of seedlings which increases their chance of reaching light. What would happen to seedlings which did not reach suitable light conditions? Explain your answer.

2. The diagrams below show an experiment on the phototropic responses of young plant shoots.

Step 1 – shoot tip removed and placed on an agar block and illuminated from one side.

Step 2 – agar block placed on cut end of shoot and illuminated from above.

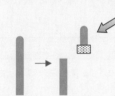

shoot grows in a curve

   (a) What evidence from the experiment suggests that the substance responsible for the uneven growth of the shoot moves from the shoot tip to the area of cell elongation by diffusion?
   (b) What evidence from the experiment suggests that the distribution of the substance responsible for the uneven growth of the shoot becomes unequal between the illuminated and the shaded side of the shoot?

3. Cocklebur is a flowering plant whose flowering is initiated by changes in the photoperiod. Cocklebur plants were kept in controlled conditions in which the photoperiods could be controlled. The diagrams below represent the hours of light and dark received by the plants in each twenty-four-hour period, together with the effect on the flowering of the plants.

Plant 1	15 hours' light / 9 hours'	no flowers
Plant 2	14·5 hours' light / 9·5 hours' dark	no flowers
Plant 3	14 hours' light / 10 hours' dark	flowers
Plant 4	14 hours' light / 10 hours' dark	no flowers

darkness interrupted
by flash of light

   (a) Is cocklebur a long-day or a short-day plant with respect to its flowering? Give a reason for your answer.
   (b) What is the critical period for cocklebur?
   (c) What evidence suggests that the length of darkness is more important than the length of light in initiating flowering?

The principle of negative feedback

The need to maintain conditions within tolerable limits

The cells of the body function as a result of the chemical reactions which take place in them. These reactions are controlled by enzymes which are affected by factors such as temperature, pH, concentration of their substrates and the water concentration of the solution they work in. It is important that these conditions remain as stable as possible inside the body, in spite of changes in the outside environment. In many cases the body regulates its internal conditions by negative feedback systems. The maintaining of constant conditions in the body is called **homeostasis**.

A **negative feedback** system provides automatic control of a factor. Any change away from the norm is detected by receptors which switch on a corrective mechanism which causes conditions to return to normal. Once the conditions have returned to normal, the corrective mechanism is switched off.

Many negative feedback systems of the body involve the use of hormones. Hormones are chemicals that are produced by various glands in the body and then transported in the blood to where they cause a response.

Temperature

Mammals and birds have the ability to maintain a constant body temperature, despite temperature variations of their surroundings. This is advantageous because it ensures a constant internal environment at an optimum temperature for enzyme-controlled reactions.

Heat is generated within the body and is lost to the surroundings. The hypothalamus monitors the temperature of the blood flowing through it and it also receives nerve signals from temperature receptors in the skin. Variation in body temperature triggers nerve signals from the hypothalamus to a number of structures in the body. These structures respond and their actions bring the body temperature back to normal.

The skin has several adaptations involved in temperature control:

- Surface blood vessels can become wider (**vasodilation**) or narrower (**vasoconstriction**) to allow more or less blood to flow near the skin surface. This will increase or decrease heat lost by radiation.
- Sweat glands increase or decrease the production of sweat. Sweat evaporates from the skin and removes heat as it does so. Therefore an increase or decrease in sweating will increase or decrease heat loss.
- Erector muscles attached to hairs lower or raise the hairs. This decreases or increases the insulating effect of trapped air near the skin surface and so increases or decreases heat loss.

Some of the muscles may begin shivering as a means of increasing heat production in the body.

The metabolic rate can also be adjusted to increase or decrease heat production.

The mechanisms involved are shown in the diagram.

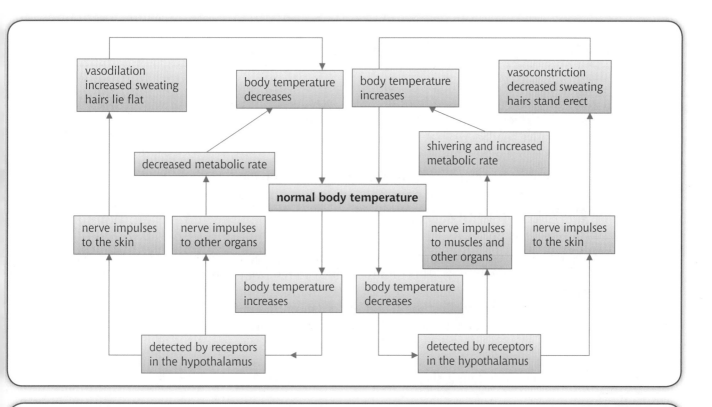

Endotherms and ectotherms

A negative feedback mechanism for controlling temperature can only work for an animal that is capable of generating enough heat to maintain a constant body temperature above that of its surroundings. Such animals are called **endotherms**. Mammals and birds are endotherms.

Animals which derive most of their heat from their surroundings, rather than by their metabolism, are called **ectotherms**. Such animals do not regulate their temperature to the same extent as endotherms. Instead, their body temperature varies according to the temperature of their surroundings. They will try to avoid excessive changes in temperature by behavioural means such as hiding in the shade to avoid overheating and lying in the sun to warm up. Reptiles, amphibians and fish are ectotherms.

Top Tip

If you are asked to describe a negative feedback system, remember to include the location of the receptors involved in detecting the changes.

Quick Test 35

1. The diagram shows part of the mechanism which regulates body temperature.

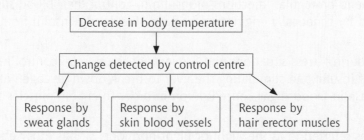

(a) (i) Name the control centre involved in this mechanism.
   (ii) How does the control centre pass instructions to the effectors in the skin?
   (iii) Describe the response of the three effectors mentioned and explain how each contributes to conserving body heat.
(b) Describe one additional response which may take place as a result of a decrease in body temperature.

Glucose and energy needs of tissues

Every cell of the body uses glucose from the blood as a respiratory substrate. The blood gains glucose by absorption from the small intestine. This has the potential to cause a sudden rise in the blood sugar concentration but this is controlled by a negative feedback system which causes the removal of glucose from the blood and into the liver for temporary storage.

The system involves three hormones, **insulin**, **glucagon** and **adrenaline**. Insulin and glucagon are both produced by the **pancreas**. Adrenaline is produced by the **adrenal glands** near the kidneys.

The liver stores glucose as **glycogen.**

The negative feedback system involves the release of insulin from the pancreas if the blood sugar concentration rises. This causes the liver to remove glucose from the blood and convert it to glycogen. It also causes the cells of the body to take in more glucose from the blood. If the blood sugar concentration falls, the pancreas releases glucagon instead of insulin. This causes the liver to breakdown glycogen and release glucose into the blood. The pancreas is responsible for monitoring the blood sugar concentration and then releasing the appropriate hormone. The homeostatic system is shown in the diagram below.

Top Tip

These homeostatic processes are described as negative feedback systems because the response to a change in conditions produces a negative effect. In other words, the response causes an effect which is the opposite of the initial change.

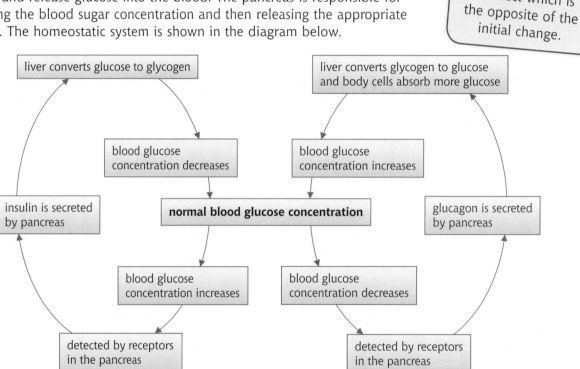

The pancreas of some people does not produce insulin. They suffer from the most severe form of **diabetes** and they depend on regular injections of insulin to control their blood sugar levels. Human insulin is now produced by genetically engineered bacteria. Previously, insulin from slaughtered animals had to be used.

Adrenaline is released during stress situations and it overrides the normal control mechanism by inhibiting the release of insulin and stimulating the liver to break down glycogen and release glucose. This results in an increase in blood sugar concentration in order to enable muscles to work efficiently if required.

Adrenaline is sometimes referred to as the 'fight or flight hormone'. It has other effects connected with the sudden need for physical action.

Water concentration of the blood and concentration of cell chemicals

The kidneys are the organs which maintain the water balance of the body. They do this by adjusting the reabsorption of water from the kidney tubules back into the blood to maintain the water concentration of the blood within its correct limits.

The water concentration of the blood can vary according to the water gains and losses of the body. The blood water concentration is monitored by **osmoreceptors** in the **hypothalamus** at the base of the brain.

The hypothalamus regulates the release of the hormone **ADH** (antidiuretic hormone) from the **pituitary gland**. If blood water concentration is low then more ADH will be released by the pituitary gland. If blood water concentration is high, then less ADH will be released.

If ADH is present in the blood passing through the kidneys, the permeability of the tubules and the collecting ducts is increased. This allows more water to be reabsorbed from the glomerular filtrate back into the blood. This increases the water concentration of the blood. The system is shown in the diagram.

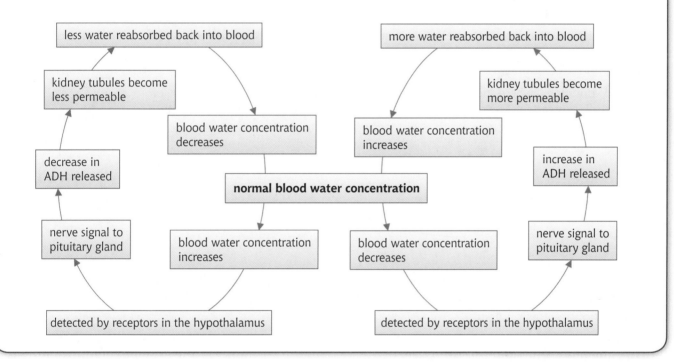

Quick Test 36

1. Give an account of the principle of negative feedback with reference to the maintenance of blood sugar levels.

Regulation of plant and animal populations 1

Population fluctuations

Populations can be considered on various scales from the global population of a species to smaller groups found in local habitats. Normally a **population** is considered to be an interbreeding group of organisms of the same species, within the same habitat.

The size of a population is affected by several factors:

- **The birth rate** – this is usually expressed as the number of births per 1000 of the population in one year.
- **The death rate** – the number of deaths per 1000 of the population in one year.
- **Immigration** – this is a measure of new individuals entering the population from other areas.
- **Emigration** – a measure of individuals leaving the population and moving to a new area.

A population will increase if the additions from births and immigration are greater than the losses by death and emigration.

In a well-balanced ecosystem, the population size of most species is relatively stable, although it is subject to short-term changes. These fluctuations are due to variations in factors such as temperature, disease and food supply.

In ideal conditions, where there is no restriction of food or space and no predators or disease, all populations have the potential to grow at an increasing rate. This situation would result in a growth curve for the population similar to the one shown below.

Top Tip

Notice that in exponential growth the time taken for the population to double becomes less and less.

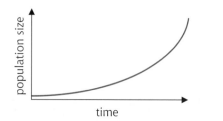

This is known as exponential growth and it cannot be maintained indefinitely. At some point the population size levels out as environmental conditions limit further increase. This is called the **carrying capacity** of the environment.

This pattern can be seen in the following graph, which shows the number of sheep in the island of Tasmania since their introduction by settlers.

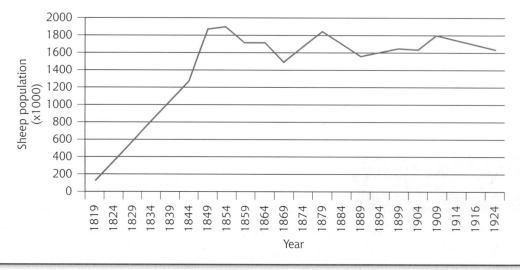

If the human population is shown on a graph, it appears that either it has not been subject to natural restrictions, or that any such restrictions have been overcome. It is obvious that the human population cannot continue to increase without limitations. The question is – will the factors which eventually restrict further population growth be planned measures, or will they be catastrophic in nature?

World Population Growth

After taking all of human history for population to reach one billion, it took only a little over a century to reach two billion in 1930. The third billion was added in just 30 years, the fourth in only 15 years.

2000	
6 billion	6 billion
1987	
5 billion	5 billion
1975	
4 billion	4 billion
1960	
4 billion	3 billion
1930	
2 billion	2 billion
1800	
1 billion	1 billion

10 000 BC
5 million

Year 1
250 million

10 000 BC   5000 BC   Year 1 1000 2000

Factors affecting population change

The fact that populations have the potential of producing far more offspring than can be sustained by the environment is one of the principles of evolution by natural selection. It is the capacity for over-production which creates the intraspecific competition that leads to the selection of particular individuals.

Factors which can affect population size fall into two categories:

- **Density-independent factors** – These factors show their effect without any variation due to population density. They include factors such as extremes of temperature, droughts, extremely high rainfall and other exceptional climatic circumstances. The chance of any individual dying as a result of the situation is not affected by the population density being high or low.
- **Density-dependent factors** – These factors vary in their effect depending on whether the population density is high or low. They have an increasing effect as the population density increases. Such factors include predation, disease and competition for food and other resources . At low population densities, these factors have less influence on population size than if there is a high population density. At high population densities predators are more likely to find their prey; food supplies may be limited, resulting in starvation; disease will spread faster and competition for resources will be more intense.

Quick Test 37

1. Various factors have an effect on the size of a population.
   The flowchart outlines how population density may be regulated.

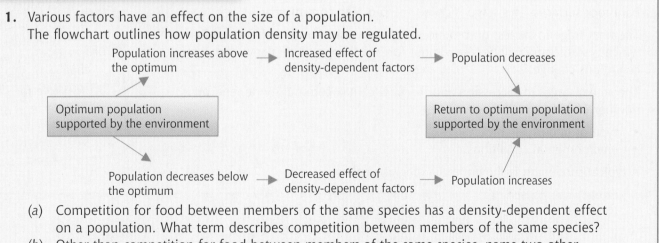

   (a) Competition for food between members of the same species has a density-dependent effect on a population. What term describes competition between members of the same species?
   (b) Other than competition for food between members of the same species, name two other density-dependent factors that affect population size, and explain how each factor has its effect.

Regulation of plant and animal populations 2

Monitoring populations

The need to monitor populations of plants and animals is becoming more important as knowledge of human impact on the environment increases.

Populations are monitored for a number of reasons:

- to ensure continued supplies of species we rely on for food or raw materials
- to be aware of pest species so that effective control measures can be introduced when needed
- as a measure of pollution levels by the presence of indicator species
- to determine whether a species is in danger of extinction and whether conservation measures are needed.

Succession and climax in plant communities

Given enough time and suitable conditions, any barren area will be colonised by plants. This is true for an untended field and for bare rock. Colonisation by plants takes place in a **succession** of stages which show increasing complexity.

The **colonisation** of bare rock is a slow process. It requires the formation of an increasingly complex soil structure from weathered rock fragments and the organic remains of simple plants before more complex plant species can become established. The colonisation of bare land that already has soil takes place over a much shorter timescale.

Each stage in the succession changes the habitat in such a way that it allows colonisation by the community of plants of the next stage. The stages always take place in the same direction and they are characterised by:

- increasing fertility of soils
- increasing species diversity
- increasing biomass
- increasing complexity of food webs.

The initial colonisers in most cases are lichens which are capable of growing on bare rock surfaces. This stage is called the **pioneer community**.

The final stage in succession produces a **climax community**, often woodland, which is stable and will persist without further change, unless environmental conditions change.

The actual stages in succession and the final climax community depend on a number of factors including:

- type of underlying rock
- environmental conditions.

A typical succession is shown in the diagram below.

Top Tip

Remember, the causes of succession are the changes to the environment that each stage brings about. These changes make it possible for a different range of plants to become established.

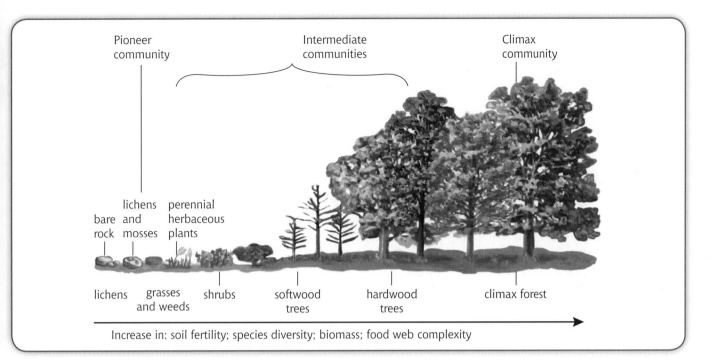

Increase in: soil fertility; species diversity; biomass; food web complexity

Quick Test 38

1. After an area of farmland was abandoned it was colonised initially by herbs and grasses. In the following eighty years there were changes in the plant community, as shown in the graphs below. Changes in the depth of organic material in the soil are also shown.

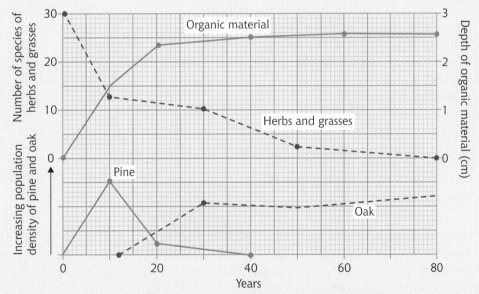

(a) What evidence in the data indicates that succession has taken place?

(b) Oak seeds can only germinate if there is enough organic material to protect them from drying out.
On the basis of the data given, what is the minimum depth of organic material required by the oak seeds?

(c) Oak woodland forms the final community of this succession.
State the name given to this community and describe a feature of such a community.

Unit 1 – Cell Biology

Quick Test 1

1. Unicellular organisms consist of one cell. Multicellular organisms contain more than one cell.
2. It allows easier translocation of the products of photosynthesis such as glucose.
3. They can distinguish light from dark and therefore remain in the light where they can photosynthesise.

Quick Test 2

1. (a) As the oxygen concentration rises, more respiration can take place and more ATP is produced. This allows more active uptake of potassium.
   (b) Oxygen is no longer the limiting factor, something else is. Therefore further increases in oxygen have no effect on potassium uptake.
2. (a) X – phospholipid   Z – protein
   (b) It is a protein which forms a channel allowing small molecules to pass across the membrane.

Quick Test 3

1. Answer D
2. (a) Chlorophyll/chlorophyll a
   (b) They broaden the absorption spectrum by absorbing other wavelengths of light and passing the energy to chlorophyll a to be used in photosynthesis.

Quick Test 4

1. (a) Hydrogen
   (b) It is part of the reduced hydrogen carrier NADPH.
   (c) To reduce the compound GP as part of the reduction of carbon dioxide.
2. (a) Glucose (carbohydrate) and RuBP.
   (b) RuBP

Quick Test 5

1. It transfers chemical energy from energy-releasing reactions, such as respiration, to reactions in the cell which require energy, such as protein synthesis.
2. ATP is continually being built up and broken down, so the amount present remains relatively constant.
3. It provides a larger surface area for the reactions of the cytochrome system to take place and so allows greater production of ATP.
4. (a) Glycolysis occurs in the cytoplasm.
      Glucose is broken down to pyruvic acid.
      The breakdown is controlled by enzymes.
      There is a net gain of 2 ATP molecules from the breakdown of each glucose molecule.
      Hydrogen is released and combines with NAD to form NADH.
      Oxygen is not required for glycolysis.

      A maximum of 5 marks would be given for this part – 1 mark for any of these points.

   (b) The Krebs cycle occurs in the matrix of the mitochondrion.
      Oxygen is needed.
      A 2-carbon acetyl group is produced from the pyruvic acid.
      The acetyl group joins with coenzyme A.
      This reacts with a 4-carbon compound to form 6-carbon citric acid.
      The citric acid is converted back to the 4-carbon compound.
      Carbon dioxide is produced.
      Hydrogen is released and combines with NAD to form NADH.
      NADH transfers the hydrogen to the cytochrome system.
      The Krebs cycle is controlled by enzymes.

      A maximum of 5 marks would be given for this part – 1 mark for any of these points.

Quick Test 6

1. Enzymes (polymerase) **or** DNA template (original DNA molecule) **or** ATP
2. (a) 58%   Adenine + cytosine = 42%. Therefore thymine + guanine = 100 – 42 = 58%.
   (b) 1080   18% of original strand are cytosine. Therefore 18% of complementary strand are guanine.
      18% of 6000 = 1080

Quick Test 7

1. proline – cysteine – lysine – histidine – tyrosine – glycine – serine – asparagine – valine

Quick Test 8

1. They can reproduce **or** They pass genetic information to the next generation.
2. Proteins on the virus surface.
3. (a) (i)   As the population density increases the total volume of resin produced decreases, up to a population density of ten trees per hectare. Further increases in population density have little effect on the total volume of resin production **or**
      At low population densities, an increase in population density reduces the total volume of resin produced. At high population densities, an increase in population density has little effect.
   (ii)   3·5 cm^3 Total excluding the first day = 29·3 – 8·3 = 21 cm^3.
                    Average per day for the six days = 21/6 = 3·5 cm^3.
   (b)   Blocks holes/seals wounds/forms a protective barrier against the entry of micro-organisms/bacteria/viruses/disease.

Unit 2 – Genetics and adaptation

Quick Test 9

1. Answer A
   Gametes have half the number of chromosomes of body cells, therefore half the DNA.
   Red blood cells do not have a nucleus, therefore no DNA.
2. First meiotic division – B and C.
   Second meiotic division – A and D.

Quick Test 10

1. (a)   6 chromosomes
   (b)   12 chromatids
   (c)   6 centromeres
   (d)   3 homologous pairs of chromosomes
2. B

Answers

3. (a) 2 chiasmata

(b)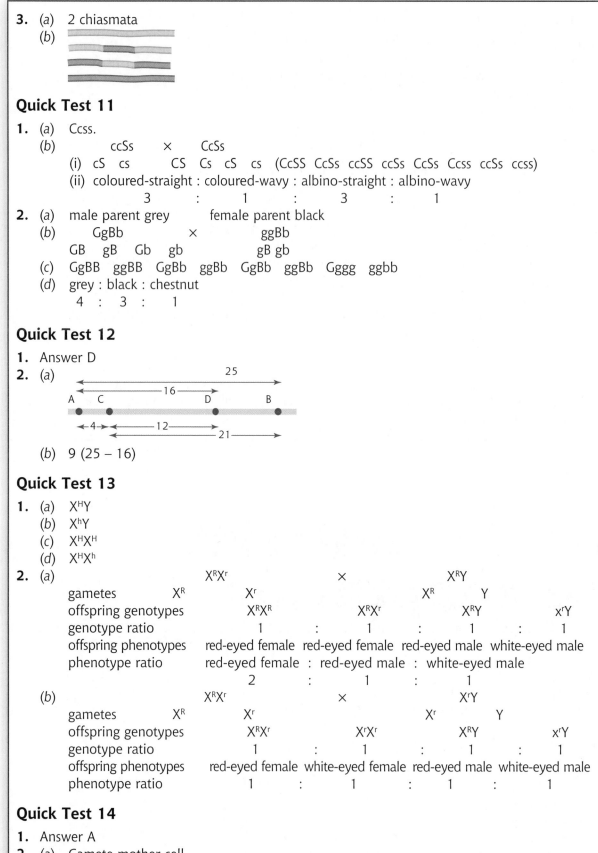

Quick Test 11

1. (a) Ccss.

(b)   ccSs   ×   CcSs

(i) cS   cs   CS   Cs   cS   cs   (CcSS CcSs ccSS ccSs CcSs Ccss ccSs ccss)

(ii) coloured-straight : coloured-wavy : albino-straight : albino-wavy

            3   :   1   :   3   :   1

2. (a) male parent grey   female parent black

(b)   GgBb   ×   ggBb

GB   gB   Gb   gb   gB gb

(c) GgBB   ggBB   GgBb   ggBb   GgBb   ggBb   Gggg   ggbb

(d) grey : black : chestnut

     4   :   3   :   1

Quick Test 12

1. Answer D

2. (a)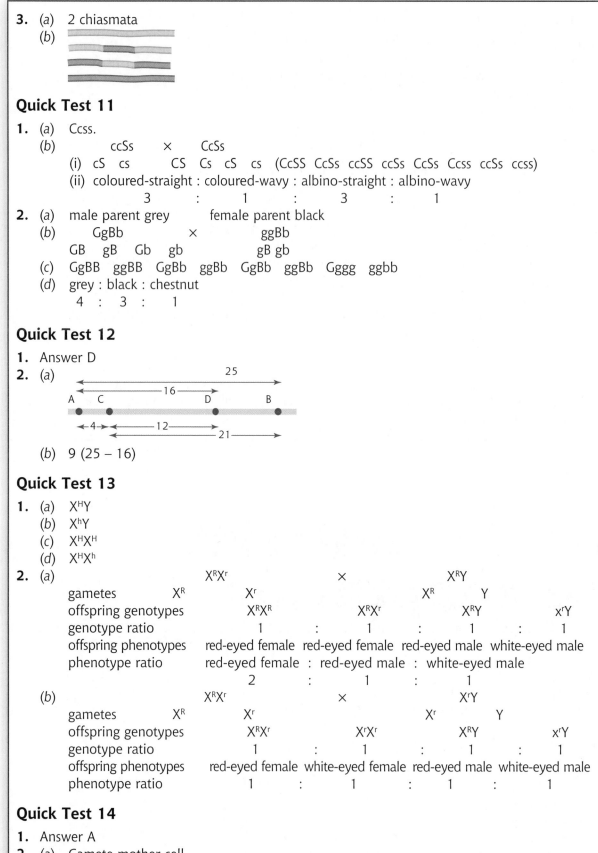

(b) 9 (25 – 16)

Quick Test 13

1. (a) X^HY

(b) X^hY

(c) X^HX^H

(d) X^HX^h

2. (a) X^RX^r × X^RY

gametes X^R X^r X^R Y

offspring genotypes X^RX^R X^RX^r X^RY x^rY

genotype ratio   1   :   1   :   1   :   1

offspring phenotypes   red-eyed female   red-eyed female   red-eyed male   white-eyed male

phenotype ratio   red-eyed female : red-eyed male : white-eyed male

            2   :   1   :   1

(b) X^RX^r × X^rY

gametes X^R X^r X^r Y

offspring genotypes X^RX^r X^rX^r X^RY x^rY

genotype ratio   1   :   1   :   1   :   1

offspring phenotypes   red-eyed female   white-eyed female   red-eyed male   white-eyed male

phenotype ratio   1   :   1   :   1   :   1

Quick Test 14

1. Answer A

2. (a) Gamete mother cell.

(b) Have the same sequence of genes **or** Have genes for the same characteristics at the same loci.

(c) Non-disjunction

(d) First division – Occurred during pairing and separation of homologous chromosomes.

(e) Two

Quick Test 15

1. (a) Translocation
   (b) Radiation **or** example (X-rays/gamma rays/UV rays)
       Chemicals **or** example (colchicine/mustard gas)
       High temperature
2. (a) Deletion
   (b) This band is missing from the mutated chromosome.

   (c) Their Y chromosome has no corresponding genes and so cannot mask the condition.
       or Males only need one mutated X chromosome to be affected. Females need two.
   (d) The missing gene means that a particular protein will not be produced or will not function
       properly.

Quick Test 16

1. Answer C – The last two bases (C and G) are inverted.
2. Insertion and deletion – because they alter every triplet of bases from the point of the mutation.
   The other gene mutations normally affect only one or two triplets.
3. (a) Inversion – an A and C have been inverted near the middle of the strand.
   (b) Substitution – a G has been substituted for a C.

Quick Test 17

1. (a) Geographical/reproductive/ecological
   (b) (i) Mutations occur randomly in each population. These produce variations between
           individuals.
           Natural selection favours different phenotypes in each population so some genes will
           increase in the population and some will decrease.
       (ii) Individuals from the two populations are unable to breed and produce fertile offspring if
            the barriers are removed.

Quick Test 18

1. Answer B
2. B A D C E
3. (a) Gene mutation alters the base sequence/genetic code of DNA.
       Results in altered amino acid sequence of protein synthesised from the DNA.
   (b) Tetracycline kills non-resistant bacteria.
       Resistant bacteria survive and reproduce, producing more bacteria that are resistant to
       tetracycline.
4. Answer B – the selection pressure is the predation by birds.
5. To preserve genetic diversity in the species **or** so that genes which may be useful are not lost.

Quick Test 19

1. Answer D
2. Contains bacterial genes   plasmid.
   Cuts DNA into fragments   restriction endonuclease.
   Locates specific genes   gene probe.
   Removes plant cell walls   cellulase.
3. Sexual incompatibility of two different species **or** the inability of different species to successfully
   interbreed.

Answers

Quick Test 20

1.

Freshwater fish	Saltwater fish
large kidney glomeruli	small kidney glomeruli
many kidney glomeruli	few kidney glomeruli
produce large volumes of urine	produce small volumes of urine
produce dilute urine	produce concentrated urine
chloride secretory cells absorb salts	chloride secretory cells excrete salts
blood hypertonic to surroundings	blood hypotonic to surroundings

2. Answer C
3. Saltwater bony fish are hypotonic to the surrounding sea water.
   They suffer a constant loss of water by osmosis, causing concentration of body fluids.
   To combat this they produce small volumes of concentrated urine. Their kidneys are adapted to do this by having a small number of small glomeruli which reduce the filtration rate.
   They also drink sea water to make up for the water loss.
   They also suffer a constant intake of salts by diffusion from gills.
   Special chloride secretory cells in the gills excrete salts by active transport to the surrounding water against the concentration gradient.

Quick Test 21

1. Provides method of transport of water, needed for photosynthesis and maintaining turgor, upwards in xylem **or** provides method of transport of essential minerals in xylem **or** the evaporation of water cools the leaves.   Any two
2. (a) Transpiration pull
   (b) Adhesion/cohesion/root pressure   Any two
3. Light intensity

Quick Test 22

1. (a)

   Transpiration rate increased by increases in:
   $\left\{\begin{array}{l}\text{temperature}\\\text{wind speed}\\\text{light intensity}\\\text{availability of soil water}\end{array}\right.$

   Transpiration rate decreased by increases in:
   $\left\{\begin{array}{l}\text{humidity}\\\text{air pressure}\\\text{pollution which blocks}\\\text{stomata}\end{array}\right.$

   A maximum of 5 marks would be given for this part – 1 mark for any of these points.

   (b) Reduced leaf size/reduced leaf number/leaves reduced to spines.
   Reduced number of stomata.
   Thick or waxy cuticle reduces water loss.
   Rolled leaves protect stomata from air movement.
   Hairs on leaf protect stomata from air movement.
   Sunken stomata protect them from air movement.
   Reversed stomatal rhythm, so stomata closed during day.

   A maximum of 5 marks would be given for this part – 1 mark for any of these points.

2. (a) Xylem not needed to transport water throughout plant.
   Plant needs less support because of surrounding water.
   (b) Having any xylem as part of a central bundle increases flexibility of the stem, so less likely to be damaged by movement of surrounding water.

Quick Test 23

1. (a) As the wildebeest age increases, the duration of successful chases increases.
   (b) Calves cannot run as fast as adults/Calves have less experience of predators/Calves are weaker than adults/Calves are less able to defend themselves than adults.
   (c) Greater overall gain in energy from catching one large prey than several smaller ones.
   (d) Able to tackle larger prey/All pack members gain food/Increases hunting success/Able to tire prey/Able to defend the kill better.
   (e) Interspecific
2. Plants make food by photosynthesis. They do not need to move to find food.
3. 4 a.m.
4. (a) Shade plants
   (b) Light from the red and blue ends of the spectrum has already been absorbed by taller plants above them.
   (c) They possess more accessory pigments able to absorb these wavelengths.

Quick Test 24

1. Answer C
2. Answer D
3. (a) (i) Nests are less accessible to predators/Chicks remain in nest and so are less vulnerable/ Crowding gives protection by neighbours.
       (ii) Eggs are camouflaged against pebbles/Three eggs increases chance of one surviving/Chicks spread out by moving from nest so are less likely to be found.
   (b) Reduced chance of any individual being attacked/Earlier detection of predators/Possible cooperative defensive behaviour.

Quick Test 25

1. 1. Meristems or growing points at the base of the stems are not eaten by grazing animals.
   2. Underground stems able to produce new leaves.
2. 1. Flattened leaves are missed by grazing animals.
   2. Leaves do not overlap so all can receive light for photosynthesis.
3. 1. Reduced surface area for loss of water by transpiration.
   2. Protect water stored in stem from animals.

Unit 3 – Control and regulation

Quick Test 26

1. (a) This is where newly formed cells elongate to full size and cause the root to lengthen.
   (b) Region C
   (c) This region contains cells that have already reached full size and so there is no further increase In length.
2. (a) L
   (b) Xylem
   (c) Spring – the latest xylem vessels produced have a wider diameter.

Answers

Quick Test 27

1. (a) It avoids the effect of variable water content/It provides a more accurate measure of the increase in mass due to photosynthesis.
   (b) It involves killing the plant by drying it.
   (c) The dry mass of samples of the plant are measured at different stages of growth and average values calculated.
2. Pea plant – Graph B; Dog – Graph C; Ladybird beetle – Graph A; Oak tree – Graph D.

Quick Test 28

1. (a)

	Lactose present	Lactose absent
(i)	True	True
(ii)	True	False
(iii)	False	True
(iv)	True	False
(v)	True	False

   (b) Lactose
   (c) They do not waste energy or resources such as amino acids by producing the enzyme until it is needed.

Quick Test 29

1. Answer C
2. Answer B
3. The concentration of phenylalanine will increase.
   The concentration of tyrosine will decrease.

Quick Test 30

1. (a) Pituitary gland
   (b) (i) Thyroxine increases metabolic rate. Group B rats have the highest thyroxine levels and will have the highest metabolic rate, leading to increased oxygen consumption. Group C rats have the lowest thyroxine levels and will have the lowest metabolic rate, leading to decreased oxygen consumption.
       (ii) They have higher oxygen consumption than Group C rats. Therefore they have a higher metabolic rate and so must make thyroxine.
       (iii) It would be lower in Group A because there would be more inhibition of the pituitary gland by thyroxine.
       (iv) 25%   ($1.6 - 1.2 = 0.4$ $0.4/1.6 \times 100 = 25\%$)
       (v) 1. Group C rats have a lower metabolic rate, causing them to produce less heat. They show constriction of skin blood vessels, resulting in the paleness of exposed skin.
           2. Group C rats will conserve body heat by curling up.
2. The pituitary gland produces GH (growth hormone).
   GH promotes the growth of bone and muscle.
   The pituitary gland produces TSH (thyroid stimulating hormone).
   TSH stimulates the thyroid gland to produce thyroxine.
   Thyroxine increases the metabolic rate.
   (Note that this question does not ask about the negative feedback control mechanism involved.)

Quick Test 31

1. (a) 10^{-8} molar to 10^{-3} molar
   (b) Use more than two lengths of shoot tip in each solution.

    (c)   No effect

    (d)   The control shoot tips grew by an average of 2 mm. Total inhibition of growth could only prevent this growth, not make the shoots shorter than they were at the start.

    (e)   To allow time for any growth to take place.

    (f)   This is where the meristem and region of cell elongation is located.

2. As rooting powders.
As selective weedkillers.
To induce fruit formation.
To induce germination of barley for malting. ⎫ any three

Quick Test 32

1. (a)   An identical container with an oat seedling in a water culture solution with no element missing.

    (b)   To prevent algae using the mineral elements in the solutions.

    (c)   (i)   The plants lacking nitrogen and phosphorus.

           (ii) The plants lacking nitrogen and magnesium.

    (d)   Chlorophyll/chlorophyll *a*/chlorophyll *b*

    (e)   Mineral uptake involves active transport. Oxygen is needed for aerobic respiration to supply the energy/ATP required.

Quick Test 33

1.

Inhibits activity of certain enzymes	Lead
Required for the uptake of calcium from the small intestine	Vitamin D
Required for normal growth of teeth and bones	Calcium and vitamin D
Required for haemoglobin synthesis	Iron
Retards both physical growth and mental development of the human embryo	Nicotine and alcohol

2. (a)   (i)   As the concentration of placental lead increases, the average birth mass decreases.

           (ii) It inhibits the activity of enzymes.

    (b)   (i)   It disrupts the development of the limbs.

           (ii) Nicotine and alcohol.

Quick Test 34

1. They would die because they would not be able to photosynthesise and make food.

2. (a)   The substance responsible must have passed into the agar block from the tip, and from the agar block into the decapitated shoot. This can only happen by diffusion.

    (b)   The illumination of the tip from one side must have caused an unequal distribution of the substance in the agar block for the agar to cause a bending of the shoot, even though it was then being illuminated from above.

3. (a)   It is a short-day plant. Flowering is initiated when the photoperiod falls below the critical period.

    (b)   9·5 hours.

    (c)   Flowering is inhibited when the dark period is interrupted, even though the photoperiod is below the critical period.

Quick Test 35

1. (a)   (i)   The hypothalamus

           (ii) As nerve impulses

           (iii) Sweat glands – decrease in sweat production so less heat lost by evaporation of sweat.
Skin blood vessels – vasoconstriction reduces blood flow at skin surface so less heat lost as radiation.
Hair muscles contract – hairs stand erect so more insulating air is trapped at skin surface.

    (b)   Increase in metabolic rate/shivering.

Answers